THE GOSPEL TO THE JEWS

I0169350

BY

Rev. Anthony J Mucciolo

MUCCIOLO PUBLISHING

PO BOX 232

GLENOLDEN, PA. 19036

Softcover – 978-0-9858606-1-5

Published by

MUCCIOLO PUBLISHING

Glenolden, Pa. 19036

I.

A large crowd filled the Temple awaiting the Word of G-d. Present in the Temple was a priest named Zachary, a member of the priestly division of Abijah. He was chosen by lot to burn incense upon the altar of the Temple. On this day, as he ministered to the LORD, Zachary turned his eyes toward heaven; and being consumed with grief, he began to pray in earnest for the children of Israel:

> O' LORD G-d of heaven, I pray to you, our great and wonderful G-d; to the One who reserves his covenant and mercy for those who love him and keep his commandments. O' G-d, please hear my prayer! Let your eyes be open and let your ears be attentive to the prayer that your servant is praying for the children of Israel. O' please hear me! Hear me as I confess not only my own sins, but also the sins of my family and people as well. O' G-d, how we have corrupted ourselves! Every one of us have sinned! In truth, we have all rebelled against you. Every one of us have rejected your statutes, your laws, and the judgments that you have given us and commanded us to obey. Our people have committed every abomination that those nations which inhabited this land before us were known to do. O' LORD, I know that none of these things are hidden from your eyes. Surely you have looked upon the people and have witnessed every evil under the sun practiced in this great land. Homosexuality! Incest! Prostitution! Sorcery!

Idolatry! And, how many of these people openly and freely worship the gods of our enemies?

You have seen the leaders of our people and their judges taking gifts and bribes from the rich, by which they rob the poor, and pervert justice and fairness. Was it not for these abominations that you cast out the nations that inhabited this land in time past and gave it to us? O' my G-d, how ashamed I am to lift up my face toward you! It's because of our iniquities that we are over our heads in trouble. Surely, you have delivered us into the hands of our enemies because we have trusted in deceitful words and abandoned your commandments. How can I even begin to plead with you after all this?

Nevertheless, I beg you to remember your promise of long ago. You said: 'When they are in the land of their enemies, I will not reject them, neither will I abhor them so as to utterly destroy them and to break my covenant with them; for I am the LORD, their G-d. Instead, I will remember the covenant that I made with their ancestors for their sake."

Tears trickled down Zachary's face as he continued to pray.

O' LORD, did you not give the land of Canaan to us for an everlasting inheritance? Did you not intend for this land to be inhabited and enjoyed by the children of Israel alone? Yet, the Gentiles occupy our borders, devour our wealth, and even claim the birthright to the land! They have entered your sanctuary, thrown down your altars, and have set up their own profane abominations! Though Zion stretches out her hands to plead, there is no one listening; no one cares! There is no one to relieve her anguish LORD. Among all the people of the earth she has no comforter.

The blood of innocent men, women and children is poured out into the street like water! Our joy and our dancing has turned to mourning! We are doomed, LORD! Surely we are doomed! All because we have provoked you, the Holy One of Israel, with our sins. There is no one to plead for us, to turn away your anger from us. If only you would turn us back to you, LORD! O' turn us toward you and we will be turned! Truly we will be turned! Renew our days like they were in the days of old. Save us, O' G-d! Save us! Deliver us from among the heathen, that we may give thanks to your holy name and triumph in your praise.

O' if only the salvation of Israel would come to Zion! Then Jacob would rejoice and Israel could celebrate the triumph of our King.   For you are the LORD, our G-d, our G-d in heaven above and in the earth beneath. Truly there is no other: you are our G-d, and we are the sheep of your pasture! You are our G-d; and we will praise your name for all eternity! Only, be merciful to us LORD, I pray.

As Zachary was lighting the incense, he was startled by a radiant presence that illuminated the right side of the altar. Immediately, he withdrew himself and cowered in fear. Extending his arm toward Zachary the angel said, "Do not be afraid, Zachary. Your prayer has been heard. Your wife Elizabeth is going to bear you a son whom you will name, John. He will bring both of you great joy and happiness, and multitudes will rejoice at his birth, for he will be great in the eyes of the LORD. He is not to drink wine nor liquor, for he will be filled with the Holy Ghost from his mother's womb. He will precede the coming of the LORD and will go forth in the spirit and power of Elijah to turn the hearts of the fathers to the children. He will also turn the lawless to the wisdom of the just, and prepare the people for the LORD."

"How can I be sure of this?" Zachary asked. "My wife and I are very old!" To this the angel replied, "I am Gabriel; one who stands in the presence of G-d. I have been sent to speak to you and to declare these upcoming events. Now, because you did not believe my words, you will be dumb and unable to speak until these things are fulfilled." Immediately, Zachary was rendered speechless.

Meanwhile, the people were waiting for Zachary to emerge, and were wondering why it was taking him so long. When he finally did appear to them, he attempted to call out, but his voice remained mute. Realizing that he was unable to speak, they reasoned among themselves that he must have been frightened by a vision. Motioning to them with his hands, Zachary told them that the LORD had visited the children of Israel, and that he had looked on their affliction with compassion. When they came to understand what he was saying, they bowed their heads and worshipped the G-d of Israel. After fulfilling his duties in the Temple, Zachary departed for his own house. In due time, Elizabeth discovered she had conceived a child in her womb. Bewildered and somewhat embarrassed because of her age, she went into seclusion for about five months.

In a vision, I saw a fiery orb of light, much greater in size and brightness than the sun, standing off in the distance in the heavens. Its flames turned inward, toward its innermost being, as though purging or refining itself. From the midst of the orb came a thunderous voice, one that sounded like the waves of a stormy sea rushing against each other. From the midst of the fire came these words:

> Listen to this, O' house of Jacob: You who are called by the name of Israel, descendants from the tribe of Judah: You who swear by the name of the LORD and make mention of the G-d of Israel, though neither in truth, nor in righteousness. For my name's sake alone will I defer my wrath. For the sake of my praise will I hold it back from you, so as not to cut you off completely. You come near me with your mouth and honor me with your lips, but your hearts are far from me. My people worship me in vain, because their respect for me is taught by the precepts of their teachers. Therefore, I will do a work among these people that will astound them. The wisdom of their wise men shall perish, and the understanding of their prudent shall vanish away.

> I am the One who frustrates the signs of the false prophets and makes fools of fortunetellers. It is I who carries out the words of my servants and fulfills the predictions of my prophets. For I am G-d, and there is no other! Listen to me, O' Jacob and Israel my chosen. I am the First, and I am also the Last. I am the LORD who has made all things. My hand has stretched out the heavens and my right hand has laid the foundation of the earth. When I call for them, they stand up in unison. Then I saw two tremendous pillars of light and fire shoot forth from the midst of his bosom, like arms, and stand before him. Then G-d

said, "Whom shall I send?" I heard a voice from his right arm, say, "send me." Then G-d replied, "My angel will go ahead of you."

Look to me and be saved, all the ends of the earth! For I am G-d, and there is no other! I will bring forth a Branch out of the root of Jesse and my Spirit shall rest upon him: the Spirit of wisdom and understanding, the Spirit of counsel and might, the Spirit of knowledge and of the fear of the LORD. When I bring forth my servant, the Branch, I will remove the evil of the land in one day. For I will place salvation in Zion for the benefit of Israel, my glory. This is the sign that I will give you: a virgin shall conceive and bear a son, and his name will be called Immanuel. He will build a house for my name. He will be my Son and I will be his Father. I will make him my firstborn and exalt him higher than all the kings of the earth. He will say to me, 'You are my Father, my G-d, and the Rock of my Salvation.' Your government will I put in his power, and he will be a father to all the inhabitants of Jerusalem and to the house of Judah. Upon his shoulder will I lay the key to the house of David. Therefore, what he opens, no man can shut; and what he closes, no man can open. He will be famous; and his fame will extend to the ends of the earth. The Gentiles will see his virtue, and all the Kings will see his glory; and he will be called by a new name which I will name for he will be a crown of glory, a royal diadem, in the hand of the LORD.

(As the LORD was speaking, the Angel Gabriel came before the LORD and presented himself; to whom the LORD gave this command:)

Go to the daughter of Zion and say, 'Behold, your Savior is coming!' Tell them that the LORD is coming out of his place, and that he is coming down to walk upon the high places of the earth. Tell them that he is doing this because of the transgressions of Jacob and for the sins of the house of Israel. Tell them that the LORD is coming with great power, and that his own arm will rule for him. Tell them that his reward is with him, and his work is already established for him.'

As the Angel turned and sped toward the earth, G-d said:

> *"You Bethlehem Ephrata, though you are the least among the tribes of Judah, yet, out of you shall come forth the One who will be my ruler in Israel; even the One whose works began in eternity.*

The Angel Gabriel was sent to a young virgin named Mary, who was betrothed to a man by the name of Joseph, both of whom were direct descendants of the family and lineage of David. Upon entering Mary's house, the Angel saluted her, saying, "Hail Mary! You are highly blessed and favored among women for the LORD is with you." Mary was frightened at the sudden appearance of the Angel, and his words were most puzzling to her. "Don't be afraid, Mary," the angel said "you have found favor with G-d. You are going to conceive a child in your womb, and at the appointed time you will give birth to a son, to whom you will give the name, Jesus. He will be a most exceptional child; for he will be called the Son of the Most High. The Almighty will give him the throne of David his forefather, and he will reign over the house of Jacob forever. His kingdom will never end." Bewildered, Mary replied, "How will this happen, seeing that I am a virgin?" "The Holy Ghost will come upon you and the power of the Most High will envelop you," Gabriel answered. "Therefore, the Holy One that is born of you will be called the Son of G-d. With G-d, nothing is impossible. For even your cousin Elizabeth, who was once said to be barren, is now with child six months. Despite her old age, she will also bear a son." Mary replied, "I am the servant of the LORD; let it be done to me as you have spoken." Upon hearing these words, the Angel departed from her sight.

As the time approached when the Spirit of the Almighty would come upon the virgin, the hosts of heaven gathered before the LORD and began to proclaim his glory, saying:

> Ah, LORD G-d! Behold, you have made the heavens and the earth by your great power and stretched out arm, and there is nothing too hard for you. Your right hand, O' LORD, has become glorious in power. According to your name, O' G-d, so is your praise unto the ends of the earth: your right hand is full of righteousness.

> How mighty is your arm! Your hand is strong, and your right hand is exalted! The LORD is great in Zion; and you are high above all the people. You O' LORD will cause your glorious voice to be heard and will show the lighting down of your arm. O' sing to the LORD a new song! For the LORD has done great and marvelous things: your right hand and your holy arm has gotten you the victory! LORD, you have made known your salvation! You have openly shown your

righteousness in the sight of the heathen! Let Mount Zion rejoice; let the daughters of Judah be glad, because of your judgments. For this G-d is our G-d for ever and ever!

Then, in appearance like a bright star streaking across the heavens, the right arm of the LORD issued forth from the Almighty and descended upon the Virgin. Wherefore, the child that she conceived in her womb was called the - Son of G-d.

II.

Not many days later, Mary traveled into the hill country to visit Zachary and Elizabeth. As Mary approached the house, and Elizabeth heard Mary's salutation, the baby leaped in her womb, and she was immediately filled with the Holy Ghost. Then in a loud voice Elizabeth cried out saying: "Blessed are you among women, and blessed is the fruit of your womb! What is the meaning of this; that the mother of my LORD should visit me? As soon as I heard your voice, the baby leaped in my womb for joy!"

Overwhelmed by Elizabeth's reception, and filled with euphoria herself, Mary exclaimed: "My soul just magnifies the LORD, and my spirit is rejoicing in G-d my Savior! Truly, he has had concern for the low estate of his handmaid. Hereafter, all generations will call me 'Blessed' because the Mighty One has done such extraordinary things to me! His name is holy! His mercy is upon all that fear him from generation to generation! He has shown great strength with his arm! He has scattered the proud in the imagination of their hearts. He has put down mighty kings from their thrones and exalted the humble! The LORD has filled the hungry with plenty while sending the rich away empty! Truly, he has helped his servant Israel! The LORD has remembered his mercy, even the mercy that he promised our forefather Abraham and his children forever!"

When the time came for Elizabeth to deliver, her neighbors and kin gathered at her house to celebrate the birth of her child. Their festivities were filled with great joy because of the mercy the LORD had shown her in shortening her delivery. When the infant was eight days old they came together again to witness the child's circumcision. At that time the family gave him the name, 'Zachary', after his father; but his mother intervened and said: "No! He is to be named John." Taken by surprise, her relatives opposed her, saying, "There isn't anyone among our kindred that has this name!" Nevertheless, Elizabeth continued to insist that the child be named John. Unable to convince her, they turned to the child's father.

Making gestures to him with their hands, they asked him what he wanted the child to be named. Zachary asked for a writing tablet, and then wrote these words upon it: "His name is John." And when they saw this they were all filled with amazement. Suddenly, Zachary's tongue was loosed and he was filled with the Holy Ghost. Immediately, he began to praise G-d and to prophesy in a loud voice: "Blessed be the LORD G-d of Israel! For he has both visited and redeemed his people! He has raised up a horn of salvation for us in the house of his servant David!! He promised by the mouth of his holy prophets since the world began that we would be saved from our enemies, and from the hand of all that hate us. He said he would fulfill the mercy that he promised our ancestors and pledged to remember his holy covenant; the oath that he swore to our father Abraham. He swore that he would deliver us from our enemies so that we could serve him without fear in holiness and righteousness all the days of our lives! Now, we shall see it with our own eyes!"

(Turning his attention to his newborn son, Zachary continued.)

"You, child, shall be called the 'Prophet of the Most High'. For you shall precede the coming of the LORD in order to prepare his way, and to give the knowledge of salvation to his people. You will teach them that their sins can be forgiven through the tender mercies of our G-d. You will also be a light to them that sit in the shadows of death, so that their feet may be guided in the way of peace."

Zachary's words were repeated throughout all the hill country of Judea many times throughout the years, bringing awe and admiration to all who lived nearby. The people wondered what the child would grow up to be, because all who came to know John were soon convinced that the hand of the LORD rested heavily upon him; for he was restless and strong spirited. Meanwhile, Mary remained with her cousin for about three full months, both ministering to Elizabeth and the newborn child before she returned to her own home.

Unable to hide the fact that she was with child, Mary tried to explain to Joseph, her espoused husband, that she had been visited by an Angel and that she was with child by the power of the Holy Ghost. Not surprisingly, since he and Mary had not yet come together as husband and wife, Joseph doubted her faithfulness to him. Nevertheless, he was unwilling to expose her to public disgrace and humiliation. Being a righteous man, he decided to divorce her quietly. But as he pondered these things in his heart, an Angel appeared to him in a dream and said, "Joseph, son of David, don't be ashamed to take Mary for your wife. That which is conceived in her womb is of the Holy Ghost. She will give birth to a son, whom you will name Jesus; for he will save his people from their sins." When Joseph awoke from his sleep, he reflected upon the words of the Angel. Then he decided to take Mary for his wife as the angel of the LORD had said. However, Joseph was not intimate with her until after she had given birth to her firstborn Son, whom he named Jesus.

At that time Caesar Augustus issued a decree that a census be taken of the entire Roman Empire. In addition, he levied a tax upon each household. In compliance with this order, Joseph and Mary, whose ancestry was of the house of David, traveled to Bethlehem to be counted in the census and to pay the tax. As they were entering the city, the time came for Mary to deliver her child. However, since there were no room for them at the inns, they were forced to take shelter in a nearby barn. Miraculously, even before her first true pain of labor came, she delivered her firstborn Son, whom she wrapped in warm clothing and laid in a manger. Later that night, as shepherds were keeping watch over their flocks in nearby fields, they were awestruck when they saw the sky above them illuminate like the dawning of the day. When they realized that it was an Angel of the LORD appearing to them, they became deathly afraid. Seeing their fright, the angel said to them: "Don't be afraid, for I have come to bring you some great news to share with all the people! Today, in the City of David, the Savior was born; the Messiah of G-d! This is the sign whereby you will recognize him; you will find him lying in a manger wrapped in swaddling clothes." A great multitude of Angels joined the first lighting up the sky like the noon day sun, singing:

Glory to G-d in the Highest, and on earth peace and goodwill to all men! Burst into joy and let us all sing together! The LORD has comforted his people! He has redeemed Jerusalem! The LORD has made bare his holy arm in the sight of all the nations, and the entire Earth shall see the Salvation of our G-d! For unto us a child is born; a Son has been given! The government will be on his shoulders; and his name will be called Wonderful Counselor, Mighty G-d, Everlasting Father, Prince of Peace! There will be no end to the increase of his government and peace. He will reign on David's throne and over his kingdom. He will establish it, and uphold it with justice and righteousness from this time on, and forever! The LORD sent his word into Jacob and it has landed on Israel!

After the Angels departed from them, the shepherds said to one another, "Let us go to Bethlehem and see this great event which the LORD has revealed to us!" Hastily, they left the fields and went into Bethlehem where they found Mary, Joseph, and the Child, who was lying in a manger as the angel had said.

From the heavens came the word of the LORD again, saying: "Now, will I rise. Now, will I be exalted. I am the LORD. The LORD is my name, and Israel is my firstborn Son. I have made him a Witness; a Leader and a Commander to the people. The nation and Kingdom that refuses to serve Him shall surely perish. They will be utterly destroyed. Yes, I will this once, cause them to know my hand and my might, and they will surely know that my name Is the LORD."

Meanwhile, the shepherds returned to the fields praising and glorifying G-d for all they had seen and heard. They began to spread the word concerning what they had been told about the Child, much to the wonder of all who listened to them.

Eight days later, in accordance with the Law of Moses, the Child was circumcised and given the name, Jesus. Then, after the days of Mary's purification were fulfilled, she and Joseph brought Jesus to Jerusalem to present him to the LORD and to offer up a sacrifice. But, as they entered the Temple, they were quite unprepared for what they were about to experience. Simeon, who had been told by the Holy Ghost that he would not die until he had seen the LORD's Messiah, excitedly approached the unsuspecting parents. Taking the Child from his mother's arms, he lifted him up toward heaven and began to bless G-d, saying: "LORD, now let your servant die in peace, according to your word. For now, my eyes have seen your Salvation. You have presented him in the sight of all the people; to enlighten the eyes of the Gentiles, and for the glory of your people Israel!" Then Simeon, the Holy Ghost being upon him, faced Joseph and Mary and gave them his blessing, "the LORD increase you more and more, both you and your children. For you are the blessed of the LORD who made heaven and earth. This Child has been sent for the rise and fall of many in Israel, and for a sign that will be spoken against. Yes, Mary, a sword will pierce through your own soul also." As Simeon was speaking, a prophetess by the name of Anna entered the Temple and approached the holy family. She was an eighty-four-year-old widow who served G-d with fasting and prayers night and day. Fastening her eyes upon Jesus, she began to give thanks to the LORD and to bless the Child in a loud voice:

O' give thanks to the LORD, for his mercy endures forever! He has redeemed us from our enemies! He has remembered us in our humiliation! He will judge the poor of our people, save the children of the needy, and break the oppressor in pieces! They will fear him as long as the sun and moon endure, even throughout all generations. His dominion will extend from sea to sea, even to the ends of the earth! Those who live in the desert will kneel before him, and his enemies will lick the dust! The kings of Tarshish and of the isles will bring presents, and the kings of Sheba and Seba will offer gifts. Yes, every king will bow down before him, and every nation will serve him! He will save the souls of the poor and needy, and of those who have no helper when they cry! He will redeem their souls from deceit and violence, and their blood will be precious in his sight. His name will last forever! All nations will call him 'Blessed'. Praise the LORD, O' Jerusalem! Praise your G-d, O' Zion! For the LORD has done marvelous things! His right hand and his holy arm have gotten him the victory! Praise the mighty name of the LORD!

Joseph and Mary remained in Jerusalem until they had fulfilled all things in accordance with the Law of Moses. Gathering their belongings, they returned to their home in Nazareth. In the process of time, certain magi from Sheba traveled to Jerusalem searching for the Child. Upon entering the City, they began to ask many of the people: "Where is the One who was born to be the King of the Jews? We have seen his star in the East and have come to worship him." When King Herod was brought the news of the magi's inquiry, he was greatly disturbed. Fearful of appearing ignorant before the magi, he summoned all the chief priests and teachers of the Law and asked them where the Messiah was to be born. "He is to be born in Bethlehem of Judea," they replied. "For it is written by the prophet:

> And you, Bethlehem Ephrata, are not the least among the rulers of Judah. For out of you shall come the Shepherd that will lead my people Israel.

After dismissing the priests and scribes, Herod sent a servant to summon the magi to appear before him. When they arrived, he questioned them concerning the nature of the star and the exact time it had appeared. Satisfied with their answers, Herod sent them on their way to Bethlehem with this charge, "Go; search diligently for the young Child. When you find him, send me word so that I may go and worship him also." Leaving Jerusalem, the magi started out on their journey to Bethlehem, but much to their amazement, the star they had seen in the East appeared to them again and lead them in a different direction to where the young Child was.

As the Child lay sleeping, the spirit of the Almighty overshadowed him and G-d said:

> To me, my Beloved, you are a magnificent bundle of myrrh. You are so radiant and ruddy. Your hair is like the finest gold, wavy and black as a raven. You have eyes like a dove: on the surface, they appear to have been washed in milk and mounted like precious jewels. Your cheeks are like a bed of spices with the aroma of perfume. Your lips, just like the lilies, drip with droplets of sweet smelling myrrh.

I compare your arms to gold branches, and your body to polished ivory decorated with sapphires; more excellent in beauty than the cedars of Lebanon! You are incomparable among ten thousand, for my grace is poured into your lips. I will cause your name to be remembered throughout all ages, therefore, the people will praise you forever.

Arise! Shine! Your light has come, for my glory is risen upon you. Open your eyes and see how they gather themselves together and come to you now. For in this manner will your sons come from afar and your daughters will be nursed at your side. Yes, the greatest part of the earth will be converted to you. Even now, men from Sheba are coming to you, bringing gold and incense and proclaiming the praises of the LORD.

Shortly thereafter, the magi arrived at the house where Mary and the young Child lived. As soon as they saw Jesus, they prostrated themselves before him and worshiped him. Referring to the Child as the "new-born King of Israel," they lifted up their voices in praise to G-d. Then they unpacked the gifts they had brought for him, gold, frankincense and myrrh, and presented them to the "newborn King."

At the bidding of Joseph and Mary, the weary magi lodged with them for the night and were refreshed. The next morning, they left for their own land by another route, for they had been warned by G-d in a dream not to return to Herod, nor to send him word concerning the whereabouts of the Child. Joseph had also been warned by an Angel in a dream saying, "Arise; take the Child and his mother and flee to Egypt. Stay there until I bring you word to return. Herod wants to kill the Child, and is about to begin a search for him." When Joseph awoke, he quickly gathered Jesus, Mary, and all their belongings and fled into Egypt where they remained until the death of Herod. Thereby the word which the LORD spoke by Hosea, the prophet, was fulfilled saying, *'Out of Egypt have I called my son.'*

When Herod realized that he had been scorned by the magi, he was filled with rage. In his wrath, he called for his captains and ordered them to go to Bethlehem, and to all the surrounding regions of Judea, with this command: "Kill every male child that is two years old and younger." (This was the time that had elapsed since the magi had seen the star). Within days the whole land was filled with weeping and mourning, as the prophet Jeremiah had prophesied:

> *A noise was heard in Ramah; lamentation, weeping and great mourning; Rachel, weeping for her children, refuses to be comforted, because they are dead.*

Soon after, Herod and all the men who had planned to kill Jesus died. After his death, an angel of the LORD appeared to Joseph in a dream once again, saying: "Arise; take the Child and his mother and return to Israel: for all of those who searched for the Child, intending to kill him, are dead." Therefore, when Joseph awoke, he gathered his family and returned to Nazareth where the Child was weaned and grew up. Thus, another prophecy was fulfilled which says, 'He shall be called a Nazarene.'

III.

Every year, Joseph and Mary traveled to Jerusalem to observe the Passover feast, and when Jesus was twelve years old they took him with them for the first time. At the conclusion of the Feast, having fulfilled all things in accordance with the Law of Moses, they began their journey home, unaware that Jesus had stayed behind in Jerusalem. They traveled a full day's journey before realizing that Jesus was not with the company. When they began looking for him among their relatives and friends and could not find him, they anxiously started a diligent search throughout the entire caravan. But, when they were unable to locate him, the distraught parents returned to the City in desperate search for the young lad. Meanwhile, Jesus was sitting in the Temple amid the teachers and doctors of the Law, both listening to them and asking them questions. Jesus listened intently, as one of the teachers read a portion of the Scriptures:

> *Happy is the man whom G-d corrects! Therefore, do not despise the chastening of the LORD. For he makes the sore and he dresses it; he makes the wound and his hands make it whole again. Behold he takes away and who can hinder him? Who can say to him, 'What are you doing?' If G-d will not withdraw his anger, the proud are brought low before him. We have searched this out and found it to be true. Therefore, to him that is afflicted, pity should be shown from his friends.*

Then Jesus answered him and said, "I know that what you are saying is true. If only a man would plead for another with G-d, as he argues before a judge on behalf of his neighbor!" Raising his voice in utter amazement, the teacher responded, "How can I dispute with him? Though I am a righteous man, I could not respond to him! I would only be able to plead with my judge for mercy, besides, if I had summoned him, and he responded, I would not believe he had acknowledged my voice! He is not a man like me that I might be able to argue with him; or, that we might confront one another in court!

I wish there was someone to arbitrate between us! Someone who could remove G-d's rod from us, so that I would not be frightened of his judgment! Then I would certainly speak without fear to him; but, as it is now, I can't do that! Understand this: G-d's judgment is much less severe than our iniquity deserves. If he convened a court and confined you to prison, who can oppose him? Who could answer him a single word? Listen, prepare your heart and put away your sin, stretch out your hands toward him in sincerity and humility. Acquaint yourself with him, and live in peace. Then you will be able to lift up your face without shame because there is hope." His voice rising in mock dismay, Jesus answered and said, "Where is my hope? Based on what you have said, how can a man profit by praying to him? Nevertheless, speaking for myself, I would make my appeal to G-d and lay my cause before him."

"Do you mean to correct what I say?" The teacher retorted. "Can you understand the mysteries of G-d? Can you discover the boundless limits of the Almighty? Tell me! Will you argue the case on behalf of G-d? Will you show him partiality? How would it turn out if he examined you? Could you deceive him as you might deceive men? Surely, he would rebuke you if you were to show bias! We are gray-haired, elderly men, much older than your father. What do you know that we don't know? What insights can you have that we don't have?"

Then Jesus responded: I know that I am a young man and much younger than you. Therefore, I was respectful and withheld my opinion. I said to myself, 'Let the elders speak; for by reason of their age they should teach wisdom.' But, there is a spirit within a man, and by the inspiration of the Almighty they get understanding. Great men are not always wise. Neither do the elderly always have clarity in matters of judgment. The LORD our G-d has given me the tongue of the enlightened, so that I may know how to speak a word at the appropriate time to the weary. He wakes me up every morning and opens my ears to pay attention as a wise man would do. Now, I will tell you what I know. Therefore, I will ask you to listen to me, even as I listened to you when you spoke, and gave you my full attention while you considered what you were going to say. I am full of words, and because the spirit within me is compelling me, my belly feels like it is ready to burst like new wine bottles. The spirit of G-d has made me; and the breath of the Almighty has given me life. I will show partiality to no one; neither will I flatter any man.

Directing his words to one of the teachers, Jesus said, I heard you say, 'I am a righteous man; without transgressions; innocent, there is no iniquity in me;

yet, he finds fault with me.' In this, you are being unjust. I will declare to you that G-d is far greater than man. For there is no one righteous; no, not even one. For G-d does speak to man, more than once! Oftentimes, when a man is sleeping, he will speak to him in dreams and visions and seal their instructions. In this way, he gives a man the chance to reconsider, and even withdraw from his plans. By keeping him from the pitfalls of pride, G-d keeps back his soul from falling into a pit and from perishing altogether.

A man may also be punished by being confined to his bed with great pain, even constant pain. His flesh may begin to rot away so that his bones stick out as he gets closer to death. However, if there was a single messenger, one intercessor, that would declare to the man the goodness and uprightness of G-d, the man would surely pray to G-d. Then G-d would be gracious to him and say, 'Spare him from going down to the grave; I have found a ransom for him.' Then his flesh would be renewed like a child's. If the man will pray to G-d, G-d will look upon him with favor. If the man will say, 'Surely I have sinned and perverted that which is right, but it didn't profit me;' G-d will be merciful to him and deliver him, and his life will be restored. G-d does these things many times with man, though a man may never be conscious of it. He does it to save his soul from the grave, and so that he may be enlightened with the light of the living.

Certainly, it is proper to say to G-d, 'I have suffered your chastisement, I will not offend you anymore. That which I cannot see, teach me, so that I will not sin again.' Why? Because G-d is mighty, and he despises no one. If they obey and serve him, they will spend their days in prosperity, but, if they refuse to obey, they will perish and die without knowledge. Regarding the Almighty, he is perfect in justice, judgment, and power. He is mighty in strength and wisdom. He will never afflict anyone.

After searching all over Jerusalem for her son, to no avail, Mary was grief stricken. When she found Joseph she said: "I looked all over for him, but I could not find him! The city guards stopped me, and I asked them if they had seen my son; but they said they have not seen nor heard from him." Then Joseph said, "Let us go to the Temple; perhaps the LORD our G-d will direct us to him." When they entered the Temple, they were astonished to find Jesus sitting among the doctors and lawyers. As they drew near to the men, Mary said to him, "Son, why have you treated us this way? Your father and I have been searching all over for you with great sorrow." Then Jesus replied, "Why were you searching all over for me with sorrow? Did you not know that I would be about my Father's business?"

Confused by his words, but overjoyed that she had found him, Mary went up to her son, embraced him, and said, "Come back with us to Nazareth." Then he arose and returned home with them. Thus, the word of the LORD was fulfilled, saying:

> I found my son. I held him and would not let him
> go until I brought him home to my mother's house.

In the years to follow, Jesus became proficient at several crafts. However, he found his greatest satisfaction in farming and shepherding. He cherished the time that he would spend alone in the fields attending to the tender plants or shepherding the flock, because it was at these times that he would find great solace and intimacy with the Father who was ever with him. On one such day, the young lad heard the voice of the Father beckoning to him: "Here I am, speak Father." Jesus replied. "My son," G-d said, "pay very close attention to my wisdom. Preoccupy yourself with my instructions and with understanding my judgments. In this way your lips will always retain knowledge, and you will know when and how to speak. Listen to your Father, but never decline to observe the instructions of your mother. Give me your heart, and let your eyes be fashioned solely on my ways."

"O' how I love your instructions!" Jesus replied. "I will meditate upon them day and night. Your words have been true from the very beginning, and I know that every one of your judgments will endure forever. Seven times a day do I give you praise because of your righteous judgments! You have clothed me with skin and flesh and have fenced me in with bones and tissue. You have granted me this life, and your grace and visitation have preserved my spirit. I have sworn that I would uphold your righteous decrees, and I will keep my word. Praise is waiting for you in Zion, O' G-d; and my vow shall surely be fulfilled. Though I may come to riches and have an abundance of wealth, yet in all my labors, they will find no iniquity in me that may be called, 'sin'. I will praise you with my whole heart, and I will sing praises to you before the Angels because you have magnified your word above all your name!"

In the process of time Jesus purchased a field on the slope of a very fertile hill and became a farmer. Working with what appeared to be endless energy, he placed hedges around its perimeter. Then after removing the stones and tilling the ground, he built a tower and winepress in the center of the vineyard. Afterwards he fertilized the soil and planted it with seed that he had carefully selected. When all was finished, Jesus went out and hired gardeners and caretakers to work in his vineyard, and shepherds to attend to his cattle. In a short time, he amassed a very large herd of sheep and cattle, and because the Father had prospered him greatly, his name was known as far away as Egypt. Thus the Scripture was fulfilled:

> *His name spread abroad even to the entering of Egypt; for he strengthened himself exceedingly. He had much cattle, both in the low country and in the planes. He had husbandman and vine dressers in the mountains also, for he loved husbandry.*

Several years later, the Eternal Father appeared to John, the son of Zachary, as he reclined in the desert: Jesus was now about twenty-six years of age. G-d said to John,

Son of man, stand upon your feet and I will speak to you." Immediately, the Spirit entered John and gave him the strength to stand, for he was terrified. Then G-d said: "Before I formed you in the belly, I knew you. Before you were ever born, I sanctified you and ordained you to be a prophet to these people." John exclaimed, "O' LORD! I am too young to preach!" In response to these words, G-d said: "Don't say you are too young! For you will go to all that I send you, and will speak all the words that I command you to speak. Don't be afraid of their faces, for I will be with you to deliver you. I am sending you to the house of Israel. They are a defiant nation that has continuously rebelled against me. Both they, and their forefathers, have defied me to this very day. They are arrogant and hardhearted children. I am sending you to the say to them, 'Thus and thus has the LORD said.'

You will speak to them whether they want to hear it or not. They are surely a defiant people; yet they will know that there has been a prophet among them. As for you, though you dwell among scorpions, do not be afraid of them or of their words. Neither be rebellious like them. Open your mouth and eat what I give you. Speak my words to them, whether they want to hear them or not. You are not being sent to a people of a strange tongue, but to the house of Israel. If I were to send you to a people whose tongue is hard to be understood, they would surely listen to you. But, Israel will not listen to you because they would not listen to me. Every one of them are insolent and stubborn.

Listen with your ears and receive in your heart every one of my instructions. Go to your people, and speak to them, whether or not they want to hear it. Prepare yourself and go. Don't be terrified by them, or I will surely embarrass you in front of them. Tell them that I take no pleasure in the death of the wicked. Tell them to turn from their wicked ways: to repent of their evil works and live.

Then suddenly the LORD whom you seek will come to his Temple. The messenger of the covenant whom you delight in will come; for I will raise one up from among your brethren, in whose mouth I will put my words. He will speak all that I command him to speak. Yes, I will raise me up a faithful priest who will do that which is in my mind and in my heart. Whosoever will not listen to my words, which he will speak in my name, I will demand that he give an accounting. Be aware they will bind you with chains and put you in prison. I don't want you to be afraid, for I am with you. Neither be discouraged; for I am your G-d.

Distraught and bewildered, John began his journey into Judea, where he would become known as John the Baptist. He traveled all throughout Judea, preaching the word of the LORD, saying: "Repent, for the Kingdom of heaven is at hand," and baptized all who came to him in the Jordan River.

Jesus knew that the days were fast approaching when he should begin the work that he had been sent to do. Therefore, he prepared a feast and invited his brothers, sisters, and trusted servants to dine with him. After the meal, he gave them a charge to care for the poor and transferred all of his worldly substance to their keeping. Then he left them and went into his garden to pray. Calling upon the name of the LORD, Jesus said, "I know that my hour is near; but who has believed our report? To whom is the arm of the LORD revealed?" G-d answered him and said, "As it is written by the prophet: 'Behold, I am sending my messenger before your face that shall prepare the way before you.' The arm of the LORD has been revealed to the one whose voice is heard crying out in the desert saying, 'Prepare the way of the LORD and make his pathways straight.'"

The following day, Jesus journeyed beyond the Jordan and came to the village of Bethany where John was preaching. Standing at the rear of the crowd, he listened intently as the priests and Levites confronted John and demanded to know who he was. But when John saw them approaching, he cried out in a loud voice: "O' generation of vipers! Who has warned you to flee from the wrath to come? Bring forth fruit that is satisfactory for repentance. Don't say in your heart, 'We have Abraham for our father,' because I tell you that G-d is able to raise up children to Abraham out of these stones! Even now, the axe is laid to the root of the trees, and every tree that doesn't bring forth good fruit will be cut down and cast into the fire! Yes, I baptize you with water for repentance. But, there is one coming after me who is mightier than I; one whose shoes I am not even fit to carry. He will baptize you with the Holy Ghost and with fire. He is coming with a fan in his hand, and he will clear his threshing floor. He will gather the wheat into his barn and burn up the chaff with unquenchable fire."

"Who are you?" They asked. John answered, "I am not the Messiah, if that is what you want to know." "Who then? Are you Elijah?" They asked; urging him on further. He said, "I am not Elijah." Then they asked him, "Are you the prophet?" "No, I am not." He answered. Again they asked, "Who are you? Give us an answer to take back to those who sent us! What do you have to say about yourself?" John replied, "I am the voice of one crying out in the wilderness, make straight the way of the LORD, as the prophet Isaiah has said." Then they asked him again, "if you are not the Messiah, nor Elijah, why do you baptize then?" John said, "I baptize you with water but there stands one among you whom you don't know. It is he who has the preeminence over me, even though he is coming after me. I am not worthy to even stoop down and untie his shoe latchet. Nevertheless, through him all the earth shall see the salvation of our G-d!"

(Upon hearing these words, Jesus turned and went into the hills to pray).

Then the people began to pressure John even more. They asked him, "What shall we do?" "Repent!" John exclaimed. "The kingdom of heaven is close at hand! He that has two coats, let him give one to someone who doesn't have one. He that has food, let him do likewise." Then came the public officials to him and asked, "Teacher, what shall we do?" He said to them, "Don't demand more from the people than what you are required to collect." When the soldiers came to him and asked him what they needed to do, John replied, "Don't be violent with anyone. Don't accuse anyone falsely; and be content with your wages." With many more words of exhortation, John continued to preach the words that G-d had given him a charge to speak, and all who would come forward in repentance he would baptize in the name of the LORD.

The next day, as John was preaching, he saw Jesus walking toward him. Immediately, he proclaimed in the ears of the people these words: "Look! The Lamb of G-d who takes away the sins of the world! This is the one I spoke of when I said, 'After me is coming a man that is preferred before me, because he was before me'. I did not know who he was. But, the reason that I came baptizing with water was that he might be revealed to all Israel." As John was speaking, Jesus came forward to be baptized by him. But John refused saying, "I need to be baptized by you, and you come to me?" Then Jesus answered, "Permit it to be done. This is necessary for us in order that we may fulfill all righteousness." Then John took him, submerged him in the Jordan River, and baptized him in the name of the LORD. As

Jesus came up out of the water, John heard a voice from heaven, saying, "This is my beloved son, in whom I am well pleased."

When John saw the Spirit of G-d descend in the figure of a dove, and rest upon him, he gave this testimony: "I saw the Spirit come down from heaven like a dove and remain on him. I would not have known who he was accept that the One who sent me to baptize with water said to me, 'This is he.' He also said to me, 'The man upon whom you see the Spirit descend and remain is the One who will baptize with the Holy Ghost.' Therefore, I am bearing witness to what I have seen."

(Holding his hand upon the head of Jesus, John proclaimed for all to hear:) "I declare before all of you here today that this is the Son of G-d!

In the beginning was the Word and the Word was with G-d and the Word was G-d. All things were made by him; and without him was not anything made that was made. In him was life; and the life was the light of men. And the light shines in the darkness; and the darkness comprehends it not. He is the true light that lights every man that comes into the world. He is in the world, and the world was made by him, but the world knows him not. He came unto his own, and his own received him not. But as many as receive him, to them he gives the power to become the sons of G-d, even to them that believe on his name: Which were born, not of blood, nor of the will of the flesh, nor of the will of man, but of G-d. And the Word was made flesh, and dwells among us, (and we beheld his glory, the glory as of the only begotten of the Father,) full of grace and truth."

IV.

This is the genealogy of Jesus, the reputed son of Joseph. He was the son of Mary, and the grandson of Heli. Heli was the son of Matthat. Matthat was the son of Levi. Levi was the son of Melchi. Melchi was the son of Janna. Janna was the son of Joseph. Joseph was the son of Mattathias. Mattathias was the son of Amos. Amos was the son of Nahum. Nahum was the son of Esli. Esli was the son of Nagge. Nagge was the son of Maath. Maath was the son of Mattathias. Mattathias was the son of Semei. Semei was the son of Joseph. Joseph was the son of Judah. Judah was the son of Joanna. Joanna was the son of Rhesa. Rhesa was the son of Zerubabel. Zerubabel was the son of Salathiel. Salathiel was the son of Neri. Neri was the son of Melchi, Melchi was the son of Addi. Addi was the son of Cosam. Cosam was the son of Elmodam. Elmodam was the son of Er. Er was the son of Jose'. Jose' was the son of Eliezer. Eliezer was the son of Jorim. Jorim was the son of Matthat. Matthat was the son of Levi. Levi was the son of Simeon. Simeon was the son of Judah. Judah was the son of Joseph. Joseph was the son of Jonan. Jonan was the son of Eliakim. Eliakim was the son of Melea. Melea was the son of Menan. Menan was the son of Mattatha. Mattatha was the son of Nathan. Nathan was the son of David. David was the son of Jesse. Jesse was the son of Obed. Obed was the son of Boaz. Boaz was the son of Salmon. Salmon was the son of Naason, Naason was the son of Aminadab. Aminadab was the son of Aram. Aram was the son of Esrom. Esrom was the son of Phares. Phares was the son of Judah. Judah is the son of Jacob. Jacob was the son of Isaac. Isaac was the son of Abraham. Abraham was the son of Thara. Thara was the son of Nachor. Nachor was the son of Saruch. Saruch was the son of Ragau. Ragau was the son of Phalec. Phalec was the son of Heber. Heber was the son of Sala. Sala was the son of Cainan. Cainan was the son of Arphaxad. Arphaxad was the son of Shem. Shem was the son of Noah. Noah was the son of Lamech. Lamech was the son of Methusalah. Methusalah was the son of Enoch. Enoch was the son of Jared. Jared was the son of Mahalaleel. Mahalaleel was the son of Cainan. Cainan was the son of Enos. Enos was the son of Seth. Seth was the son of Adam. Adam was the son of G-d.

Jesus, now about thirty years of age and full of the Holy Ghost, was led by the Spirit to spend forty days in prayer and fasting in the wilderness. The word of the Almighty had come to him saying, "Arise, walk through the full-length and width of the land and behold all the abominations that the children of Israel practice here." After days of wandering through the land and observing all the wickedness that was practiced by the people, Jesus was consumed with grief. His Spirit was even more distressed over the many afflictions that his people were made to suffer. As it is written,

> "His soul was grieved for the misery of Israel. And
> – for the LORD saw the affliction of Israel, that it
> was very bitter.

> (Falling prostrate before the Almighty, Jesus
> began to pray in genuine earnest to the Father:)

Father, all of my desires and complaints are uncovered before you. I am troubled and bent over in mourning all day long. I am weak and heartbroken, and it is because of the restlessness of my heart that

I have sighed. O' G-d! The heathen have acquired your inheritance and defiled your holy Temple. The bodies of your servants have been given to the birds of heaven and to the wild beasts for food. They have shed their blood all around Jerusalem like water.

(Tears begin to roll down Jesus's face as he continues to pray).

O', if only my head was filled with water and my eyes were a fountain of tears, so that I might cry day and night for the slain of our people! Look upon me and see how greatly distressed I am! The elders of the people sit upon the ground and keep silent. They put dust upon their heads and clothe themselves in sackcloth while the victims of Jerusalem hang their heads down to the ground in shame. My eyes labor in tears and my insides are troubled because of their destruction. The children and infants are collapsing in the streets of the City. Listen to the cries of the daughter of our people because of their enemies! Because of the suffering of our people am I hurting. The anguish within me is most grievous; but I said, 'Truly this is a hardship that I must bear.'

My tabernacle is spoiled and all my cords are broken. I have seen all Israel scattered upon the mountains as sheep that have no shepherd! They have no teachers. Their pastors have become senseless. Not only have they not sought the mind of the LORD, but they have destroyed my vineyard. They have made it desolate because none of them care! O' woe be to the pastors that have destroyed and scattered the sheep of my pasture! My people have been lost sheep because their shepherds have caused them to go astray. They are forced to wander from place to place and their enemies devour them.

Then they say, 'We are doing nothing wrong!' Yet, all the while they fail to consider that they have sinned against the LORD and against heaven, the habitation of the LORD and the dwelling place of justice. My people are desolate because the enemy has prevailed. Zion spreads out her hands for help and there is no one to comfort her. She weeps bitterly in the night without ceasing. Among all her lovers she can find no comfort, because they have dealt deceitfully with her and have become her enemy. Surely, they are poor and foolish people for not knowing the way of the LORD, nor the judgment of their G-d.

So I said, 'I will go to their leaders and speak to them.' But they too have broken the yoke and shattered the bonds! From the least to the greatest of them, they are all greedy and deal falsely. They commit adultery, walk-in lies, and strengthen the hands of the wicked. Not one of them repents of their wickedness! To me, they are like the inhabitants of Sodom and Gomorrah. To whom shall I speak and give warning? Their ears are uncircumcised and they cannot listen! They despise the Word of the LORD and have no delight in it.

(As Jesus bowed his head in deep sorrow, he heard the voice of the Almighty saying):

I have sent you to be a tower and a fortress among my people so that you may try their ways. They are all pitiful rebels walking about with tale bearers, corrupting one another. Were they ashamed when they committed their abominations? No; they were not ashamed at all. They couldn't even blush! Listen to their cries! Is the LORD not in Zion? Is her King not in her? Why have they provoked me to anger with their carved images and strange mannerisms? You live in the midst of deception. In their deceit they refuse to know me. You see what they do in the cities of Judah and in the streets of Jerusalem. The children gather wood, the fathers kindle the fire, and the mothers knead dough to make cakes for the queen of heaven. They pour out their offerings to other G-ds to provoke me to anger. Even after she did these things I said, 'Turn back to me;' but she would not return. Go and proclaim these words to them: 'Return, O' backsliding Israel and I will not cause my anger to fall upon you. I am full of mercy and I will not retain my anger forever. Only acknowledge your iniquity; that you have transgressed against the LORD your G-d and have not obeyed my voice. Speak to them and say: 'Don't let the wise man boast of his wisdom, nor let the mighty man boast of his strength, neither let the rich glory in his wealth. If a man will boast, let him boast in this, that he understands and knows me, the LORD who exercises lovingkindness, judgment and righteousness in the earth, for I delight in these things.' It is for this reason that I have raised you up; to show my power through you, and that my name may be declared throughout all the earth. Also, against the pastors that feed our people, say to them: 'you have scattered my flock. You have driven them away and have not visited them. Therefore, I will visit you for the evil of your doings. I will gather my flock and set up shepherds over them that will feed them; and they will no longer be afraid or discouraged.'

Woe to the shepherd who has eyes to see, but fails to keep watch over the flock! Woe to the shepherd who has a mouth to speak but fails to teach them! Woe to the shepherd who leaves the flock! The sword shall be upon his arm and upon his right eye!

Prophesy against the shepherds and say: 'Woe be to the shepherds that feed themselves! Should the shepherds not feed the flock?! You have not strengthened the diseased, neither have you healed the sick. You have not bound up the injured, neither have you looked for, nor brought back, that which was lost. Instead you have ruled over them with force and cruelty. I am against the shepherds and I will require my flock at their hands.' The one who breaks everything in pieces is coming up before your face. Maintain your armaments and watch the way; fortify your power mightily.

He was there with the Father forty days and forty nights, during which he neither ate any food, nor drank any water. Therefore, when the days of fasting were over and he was hungry, the Tempter came to him and offered him a stone. "If you are the Son of G-d," the Tempter said, "command that this stone be turned into bread." "It is written," Jesus replied. "Man shall not live by bread alone, but by every word of G-d."

After this, the devil followed him up into a mountain and showed him all the kingdoms of the world in a moment of time. Then he said to Jesus, "All these kingdoms and the riches of them, I will give to you. They have been delivered to me, and are mine to give to whom I wish. Therefore, if you will worship me, all will be yours." Jesus replied, "Get behind me, Satan, for it is written: 'You shall worship the LORD, your G-d, and him only shall you serve." Then he followed Jesus to Jerusalem and as he sat by a rampart of the Temple, the Tempter said, "If you are the Son of G-d, throw yourself down from here. It is written: 'he will give his angels charge over you and keep you. They will bear you up in their hands, lest at any time you dash your foot against a stone.'" 'It is also written," Jesus retorted. "You shall not tempt the LORD your G-d." Upon hearing these words, the Tempter left him for a time.

(From where he was sitting atop the Temple, Jesus looked over the City. Tears began to swell up in his eyes as he said):

"O' Israel, how you have destroyed yourself! But, your help is in me. The days are coming in which I will perform the good things that I have promised you. I will bring health and healing to you, and I will reveal to you the abundance of peace and truth that are yours. Then I will cleanse you from all your iniquity wherein you have sinned against me. Once again, the name of this City will be a delightful name to me. It will be a City of praise and glory before all the nations of the earth, who will hear of all the good that I will do in you."

V.

The following day, as John was talking with two of his disciples, he noticed Jesus walking past. "Look," he cried, "the Lamb of G-d!" Immediately, his two disciples left him and ran after Jesus. When Jesus turned and saw them following, he stopped and said, "What is it that you are seeking?" "Teacher, where do you live?" They asked. "Come and see" Jesus replied. Then they followed him to his house and remained with him that night, because it was late in the afternoon. Now one of the two that heard John declare him to be the "Lamb of G-d "was Andrew, Simon Peter's brother. Immediately, Andrew began to search for his brother, yearning to bring him the good news. As soon as he found Peter he exclaimed: "We have found the Messiah!" Then he brought him to Jesus' house. When Jesus saw him, he said: "You are Simon, the son of Jonah, but from now on you will be known as Cephas," (which by translation means, a small stone). Afterwards, Jesus prepared a dinner for them and baked unleavened bread which they all ate.

The next day Jesus went into Galilee; and when he saw Philip, he said to him, "Follow me." Now Philip, like Andrew and Peter, was from Bethsaida. When he located his friend Nathaniel, he said to him: "We found him, the one whom Moses and the prophets wrote about in the Law and the Scriptures, Jesus of Nazareth, the son of Joseph!" Nathaniel replied, "Can any good thing come out of Nazareth?" "Come and see for yourself!" Philip exclaimed. When Jesus saw Nathaniel coming to him, he said of him: "Look! An Israelite indeed, in whom there is no treachery!" "Where do you know me from?" Nathaniel asked. Smiling, Jesus replied, "Before Philip called you, when you were sitting under the fig tree, I saw you." In utter amazement, Nathaniel shouted: "Rabbi, you are the Son of G-d! You are the king of Israel!" Then Jesus said to him: "Because I said that I saw you under the fig tree, you believe? You will see greater things than this! I tell you all the truth; Soon, you will see the heavens opened, and the angels of G-d both ascending and descending upon the Son of Man."

On the third day there was a marriage ceremony in Cana, a village in Galilee, to which Jesus, his mother, and his disciples were invited. When they ran out of wine, the mother of Jesus said to him, "They have no wine." She expected that he would send servants to the vineyard to buy wine from Jesus' servants. Then Jesus replied, "Woman, what am I to do with you? It would take more than an hour for them to go to the vineyard and return." Then Mary turned to the servants and said, "Do whatever he tells you." There were six stone water pots sitting there that held about fifteen to twenty gallons apiece, and Jesus said to the servants: "Fill these water pots with water." After they complied and filled them to the brim, he said, "Draw some out and bring it to the host of the ceremony." In obedience to his word, they drew out some water and carried it to the host. Now, when he tasted the water that had been turned into wine, the host said to the bridegroom: "Every man serves the good wine at the beginning of a feast, and after the men have drunk a lot, he serves them the worst; but you have saved the best wine until last!" This was the first miracle which Jesus performed in Cana of Galilee, manifesting his power; and his disciples believed in him.

After this, Jesus went to Capernaum accompanied by his mother, brothers and disciples, but they didn't remain there very long. The Passover was approaching and Jesus decided to celebrate the feast at Jerusalem.

Upon entering the Temple in Jerusalem, Jesus discovered that a number of merchants had set up booths in the Temple to sell what they called "consecrated" sheep, oxen and doves. He also noticed that they had set up tables to exchange "foreign" money. Gathering several small cords together, he made a scourge and began to drive all the merchants and their wares out of the Temple, both overturning their tables and scattering the coins. Then he turned to them who sold the doves and said, "Take these things out of here; and do not make my Father's house a house of merchandise!" (At this his disciples recalled that it was written, *'The zeal of your house has eaten me up.'*)

Afterwards the Jewish leaders assembled together and insisted that he tell them who gave him the authority to do these things. "Give us a sign from heaven that proves your authority to do these things!" They demanded. "Destroy this Temple," Jesus replied, "and in three days I will raise it up." Bewildered by the saying, the Jews exclaimed, "It took forty-six years to build this Temple, and you will raise it up in three days?!" Without answering, he turned away from them and went his way. For it is written: Go from the presence of a foolish man, when you cannot perceive in him the lips of knowledge. (The Temple he was referring to was his body).

While Jesus was in Jerusalem at the Passover, many believed in his name when they saw the miracles that he did. However, he did not commit himself to them, because he knew what was in their mind, and he did not want them to testify of any man. There was a certain Pharisee, a member of the Sanhedrin, named Nicodemus, who came to Jesus at night and said, "Rabbi, we know that you are a teacher sent from G-d; for no man can do these miracles that you do unless G-d is with him."

"I tell you the truth," Jesus replied. "Unless a man is born again, he cannot see the Kingdom of G-d." A perplexed Nicodemus responded, "How can a man be born when he is old? Can he enter his mother's womb the second time and be reborn?" Jesus answered,

"Most assuredly, I say to you, unless a man is born of water and of the Spirit, he cannot enter the kingdom of G-d. That which is born of the flesh is physical; and that which is born of the Spirit is spiritual. Don't marvel because I told you that you must be born again. The wind blows where it pleases, and you hear the noise, but you can neither tell where it came from nor where it is going. So it is with all those who are born of the Holy Spirit." Nicodemus asked, "How can these things be?" "Are you a teacher in Israel and you don't know these things?" Jesus asked. "I tell you the truth; we only speak of those things that we know, and testify of the things that we have seen, but you don't accept our testimony. If I have told you earthly things and you do not believe, how can you believe if I tell you of heavenly things? No one has ever ascended into heaven, except the one who came down from heaven, even the Son of Man who is from heaven. As Moses lifted up the serpent in the wilderness, even so must the Son of Man be lifted up; so that whosoever believes in him should not perish, but have eternal life. For G-d loved the world so much that he gave it his only begotten son; that whosoever would believe in him should not perish, but have everlasting life. G-d did not send his Son into the world to condemn the world; but that the world, through him, might be saved. He that believes on him is not condemned; but he that does not believe is condemned already, because he has not believed on the name of the only begotten Son of G-d. This is the condemnation: that light has come into the world; but men loved darkness rather than light, because their deeds are evil. For everyone that practices evil hates the light, neither comes to the light, lest his deeds should be reproved. But, he that practices truth comes into the light, so that it can be plainly seen that his works are done through G-d. Concerning the miracles of which you spoke; remember the words of Isaiah and let them sink into your heart and remain there."

> *Behold, I will do a marvelous work among these people; for the wisdom of their wise shall perish and the understanding of their prudent shall be hidden. And – in that day shall the deaf hear the words of the Book, and the eyes of the blind shall see out of darkness. The meek shall also increase their joy in the LORD, and the poor among men shall rejoice in the holy one of Israel; for I will place salvation in Zion for Israel my glory.*

After this, Jesus and his disciples went out into the Judean countryside where he spent some time alone with them and gave them instructions in the precepts of G-d;

> Pay close attention to my teachings, and retain them in your heart, for I will give you instruction in wisdom, justice, judgment and equity. Wisdom is the primary thing. Therefore, set your heart to learn wisdom; and with wisdom, get understanding. The fear of the LORD is the beginning of wisdom, and a knowledge of

that which is holy is understanding. Wisdom must enter your heart before you will be able to understand the principles of righteousness, judgment and equity. To begin with, you must avoid the wicked; turn away from them and walk away. These are the fools who mock at sin. They are the ones who cannot sleep unless they have planned mischief against someone. To a fool, practicing mischief is a sport, and they are not happy unless they cause someone to fall. Therefore, the wrath of G-d continually abides upon them. Furthermore, since they think it is not worthwhile to accept the teachings and counsel of G-d, and refuse to obey his words, he gives them over to a reprobate mind so they may fulfill the lustful desires of their heart. Then their hearts are filled with all forms of perverse wickedness: immorality, dishonesty, greed, fornication and depravity. The judgment of G-d is this – that such are worthy of death; and unless they repent they will surely die.

What does David ask in the Psalms: 'LORD, who may dwell in your tabernacle and who may dwell in your holy Hill?' And what was the answer of G-d?

He that walks uprightly, practices the works of righteousness, and speaks the truth in his heart. He that does not slander others with his tongue, nor casts a reproach upon his neighbor. One in whose eyes a vile person is condemned, but who gives honor to those who fear the LORD.

He that keeps his oath, even when it hurts, and is not given to change.

He that lends his money without interest, and does not accept a bribe against the innocent. He that does these things shall never be moved. The LORD's curse remains in the house of the wicked, but his blessing is in the dwelling of the just.

Wisdom is the most precious gift of G-d. All the things that you can desire cannot be compared to her. She is a tree of life to all that take hold of her, and everyone is happy that retains her because all who embrace her are brought to an honorable position.

During this time, the disciples of Jesus were baptizing many of the people that had come to them; and John was also baptizing people in Aenon, a village near Salem, at the same time, for he had not yet been cast into prison. When a dispute broke out between John's followers and the Jews concerning the rights of purification some of them came to John saying: "Rabbi, the one that was with you beyond the Jordan, the one you testified of, he is baptizing the people and they are all flocking to him." Then John answered saying: "A man can receive nothing unless it is given to him from heaven. You, yourselves, heard me say that I am not the Christ, that I am sent ahead of him. The bride belongs to the bridegroom: but the friend of the bridegroom which stands and hears him, rejoices greatly because of the bridegroom's voice, thus my joy is fulfilled. He must increase, but I must decrease. He that comes from above is above all; but he that is of the earth is earthly, and speaks of natural things. He that comes from heaven is above every one; and what he has seen and heard, he testifies of. Yet no one receives his testimony! The one who does receive his testimony has affirmed to his sealing that G-d is true. For he whom G-d has sent speaks the words of G-d; for G-d does not give his Spirit to him by measure. Understand this, the Father loves the Son and has given all things into his hand. So then, he that believes on the Son has everlasting life; and he that believes not on the Son shall not see life because the wrath of G-d abides on him. Therefore, believe in him, that you may live forever."

When the LORD was told that the Pharisees were saying that he made and baptized more disciples than John, (though he, himself, did not baptize any, only his disciples did) Jesus left Judea through the region of Samaria. He entered the town of Sichem near the plot of ground that Jacob had given his son, Joseph, the place where Jacob's well was located. Being tired from his journey, Jesus sat down by the well. It was about noon day, the time when the women came to draw water. So, it was not very long before a Samaritan woman approached the well. Jesus said to her, "Will you give me a drink?" (At this time Jesus was alone, for his disciples had gone into the city to buy food). The woman said to him: "How can you, being a Jew, ask me, a Samaritan woman, for a drink? You know the Jews have no dealings with the Samaritans!" Jesus answered her this way: "if you knew the gift of G-d, and who it was that was asking you for a drink and you would have asked him, he would have given you living water." Looking about him, the woman said: "Sir, you do not have anything to draw with, and the well is deep, so where do you have this living water? Are you greater than our father Jacob who gave us this well; who not only drank from here himself, but his children and his cattle did also?" "Whoever drinks of this water will become thirsty again," Jesus replied. "But, whoever drinks of the water that I give him will never thirst again; for the water that I give shall be a well of water within himself, springing up into everlasting life." The Samaritan woman said to him: "Sir, give me this water so that I won't get thirsty, nor have to come back here and draw water again." Then Jesus said to her: "Go, get your husband and return here." "I haven't got a husband," she replied. "You are correct when you say that you don't have a husband," Jesus said. "The fact is you have had five husbands, and the man you are now living with is not your husband; so what you have just said is quite true." Somewhat embarrassed and irritated at him, she replied, "Sir, I can see that you are a prophet; but our fathers worshiped in this mountain, and you Jews say that Jerusalem is the place where we must worship." "Woman, believe me," Jesus said. "The hour is soon coming when you will not be able to worship the Father in this mountain, nor at Jerusalem. You Samaritans don't know whom you worship, but we know the one whom we worship; for salvation is of the Jews. But the time is coming, and is already here, when the true worshipers will worship the Father in spirit and in truth; for they are the kind of worshipers that the Father desires. G-d is a Spirit: and those who worship him must worship him in Spirit and in truth." The woman's response to these words were filled with contempt and indignation, "I know that the Messiah is coming," she said, "the one who they call Christ; and when he comes, he will explain everything to us!" Then Jesus said to her, "I, the one who is speaking to you, am he."

Just as he finished saying these words, his disciples returned and were much surprised to find him talking with the woman. Nevertheless, no one dared ask him, "What are you looking for," or, "why are you talking with her?" Immediately, the woman left her water pot, went into the city, and said to the people: "Come, see a man who told me everything I ever did; could this be the Christ?" Then the men left the city and went out to greet him. In the meantime, his disciples urged him to eat something; but Jesus said to them, "I have food to eat that you don't know anything about." Upon hearing these words, they began to question one another to know who had brought him something to eat. "My food," said Jesus, "is to do the will of him who sent me, and to finish his work.

"Would you not say that there are yet four months before the harvest? Listen to what I am saying: open your eyes and look at the fields! They are ripe for the harvest already. The reaper is drawing his wages, and is even now harvesting the crop unto eternal life; so that both the one who plants and the one who reaps may rejoice together. Therefore, the saying, 'one plants and another harvests,' is true. I sent you to harvest that which you have not worked for. Others have done the hard work, and you have benefited by their labor."

Many of the Samaritans in that city believed in him because of this testimony of the woman: "He told me everything I ever did!" So when the Samaritans came to him, they urged him to stay. He was obliging and remained there for two days, during which time many more of the Samaritans became believers because of his teachings. These said to the woman: "Now we believe, not just because of what you said, but because we heard him ourselves and know that he is the Christ, the Savior of the world."

After two days, Jesus left Samaria and returned to Galilee where he would testify that a prophet has no honor in his own country. But when he entered Galilee, the Galileans welcomed him gladly, for they had seen all that he had done at the Passover feast in Jerusalem. A couple of days later, he decided to visit Cana again, where he had turned the water into wine. At Cana, there was a certain nobleman whose son was sick in Capernaum. When he heard that Jesus had returned to Galilee he went to him and asked if he would go down to Capernaum with him and heal his son because he was near death. Then Jesus said to him, "Unless you people see signs and wonders you will not believe." Nevertheless, the nobleman pleaded with him saying, "Sir, please come down before my child dies!" When Jesus said, "Go on home; your son is going to live," the man believed the words of Jesus and returned home.

On the way to Capernaum, his servants met him and told him that his son was alive and well. He inquired of the time of day his son began to feel better, and they replied, "Yesterday about the seventh hour the fever left him." So the father knew that it was in the same hour that Jesus said to him: "Your son is going to live." Therefore, he, and all his household, believed on him. This was the second miracle that Jesus did after coming out of Judea into Galilee.

When Jesus heard that John had been imprisoned, he went to Nazareth where he had been brought up. On the Sabbath, he went to the synagogue. When he stood up to read, the minister handed him the book of the prophet Isaiah. He opened the book and found the place where the following was written, and began to read:

> *The Spirit of the LORD is upon me, because he has anointed me to preach the gospel to the poor. He has sent me to heal the brokenhearted. To preach deliverance to the captives and the recovery of sight to the blind; to set at liberty those who are*

oppressed and to preach the acceptable year of the LORD.

Then he closed the book, gave it back to the minister and sat down. Now that everyone's eyes were fastened on him, he began to say, "Today, this Scripture is fulfilled in your hearing." As soon as he said this, the crowd began to murmur and whisper. Everyone spoke well of him but they could not help but wonder about the words he had spoken. "Is this not Joseph's son?" They asked. When all was quiet Jesus continued, "Surely you will quote this proverb to me: 'physician, heal yourself! Do here in your homeland what we have heard that you have done in Capernaum.' But, I tell you the truth, no prophet is accepted in his own land. I assure you that there were many widows in Israel in the days of Elijah, when the heavens were shut up for three and one half years and great famine prevailed throughout the land. But, Elijah was sent to none of them except to a woman of Sarepta, a city in Sidon. There were many lepers in Israel in the time of Elisha the prophet. Yet, not one of them were cleansed except Naaman, the Syrian."

When all the people in the synagogue heard these words, they were filled with anger. They rose up against him and led him out of the town to the edge of the hill, upon which the city was built, intending to throw him down headfirst. Miraculously, Jesus escaped from them and went his way. Leaving Nazareth, he went to live in Capernaum, a city on the seacoast bordering Zebulun and Naftali that it might be fulfilled which was spoken by the prophet Isaiah who said:

The land of Zebulun and the land of Naftali by the way of the sea, beyond Jordan, Galilee of the Gentiles. The people that sat in darkness have seen a great light. They that dwell in the land of the shadow of death, upon them has the light shined.

From that time on Jesus began to preach and to say: "Repent for the Kingdom of heaven is at hand." As he walked by the Sea of Galilee, he saw Simon and Andrew casting a net into the sea, for they were fishermen. He called out to them and said: "Follow me and I will make you fishers of men!" Immediately, they left their nets and followed him. Going on from there, he saw two other brothers, James and John, the sons of Zebedee, in a ship with their father mending the nets. He called out to them also, and immediately, they left their nets and their father and followed him. Continuing on his travels, Jesus journeyed throughout all of Galilee, teaching in their synagogues, preaching the gospel of the kingdom, and healing all sickness and disease among the people.

As he entered one of the synagogues he encountered a man who was possessed with an unclean spirit. Immediately, he began to scream out at Jesus saying: "Leave us alone! What do we have to do with you, Jesus of Nazareth? Have you come to destroy us? I know who you are, the Holy One of G-d!" Jesus rebuked him, saying: "Hold your peace, and come out of him!" After the devil threw the man into the midst of the crowd, he came out of him without hurting him. When the people saw this, they were filled with astonishment and exclaimed, "What a word! With authority and power he commands even the unclean spirits and they come out!" Therefore, the fame of him continued to spread throughout the surrounding regions.

As the sun was setting, the people brought their sick and those afflicted with various types of disease; and he laid his hands on every one of them and healed them. Moreover, Devils came out of many, shouting, "You are the Christ, the Son of G-d!" But, he rebuked them and would not allow them to speak, for they knew that he was the Christ.

The following day, Jesus went into a solitary place, but the people searched him out. When they reached the place where he was, they began to plead with him not to leave. In an apologetic tone, he said, "I must preach the Kingdom of G-d to other cities also. It is for this reason that I was sent here." His fame spread as far away as Syria. When the Syrians heard of him they also came into Galilee bringing their sick and those tormented with various diseases. They even brought the lunatics, and those possessed with devils, and he healed them all. As a result, multitudes were gathered to him, not only from Galilee, but also from Decapolis., Jerusalem, Judea, and from the regions beyond the Jordan; and they spread his fame as they went.

VI.

When Jesus saw the multitudes increasing, he went up into a nearby hillside. Then after he had positioned himself, he summoned his disciples, whom, after they came to him asked, "Master, we would like to ask you something. Why do the wicked prosper in their ways? Why is it that those who are evil and deceitful appear to be so happy? It seems like the unG-dly are the only ones who get rich in this world." Then Jesus advised them that he was aware of the wickedness of man, saying, "My eyes are upon all their ways, their iniquity is not hidden from me. "

If you are envious of those who oppress the weak, can it not be said that you are in agreement with their works? Don't follow in their ways; for the crooked are an abomination to the LORD. In due time they will be cut down like the grass, and wither away like a green herb on a hot day. Put your trust in the LORD and do what is good, for his secrets are revealed to those who practice works of love and righteousness, not iniquity. Let your joy be found in him: commit your life to him, and he will give you the desires of your heart. The curse of the LORD remains in the house of the wicked, but his blessings are in the house of the just. It is written: 'Blessed is everyone that fears the LORD and walks in his ways.'" Then they said to him, "Will you give us your blessing?" Jesus answered them saying:

Those who are poor in spirit are blessed: their blessing is the Kingdom of Heaven.

Those who mourn are blessed; for they will be comforted.

The meek are blessed; for they will inherit the earth.

Those who hunger and thirst after righteousness are blessed; for they will be filled.

Those who are merciful are blessed; for they will obtain mercy.

The pure in heart are blessed; for they will see G-d.

The peacemakers, they too are blessed; for they will be called the children of G-d.

Blessed are those who are persecuted for righteousness sake; for their blessing is the Kingdom of Heaven.

You are blessed when men criticize and persecute you, and say all manner of evil against you, falsely, for my name's sake.

When this happens rejoice and be exceedingly glad, for your reward is great in heaven; for in like manner did they persecute the prophets that came before you.

You are the salt of the earth: but if the salt has lost its taste, how can it be salted again? It is good for nothing, but to be cast out and stepped on by men.

You are the light of the world. A city that is situated on a hill cannot be hidden. Neither do men light a candle and put it under a bushel, but on a candlestick, so that it gives light to all that are in the house. Therefore, let your light so shine before men, so that they may see your good works and glorify your Father in heaven.

Don't think that I have come to destroy the Law or the prophets; for I did not come to destroy, but to fulfill. For truly I say to you, until heaven and earth passes away, one jot or one tittle shall not pass from the Law until it is completely fulfilled.

Therefore, whoever breaks one of the least of all my commandments and teaches others to do so shall be called the least in the Kingdom of Heaven. But, whosoever will practice them, and teach them, will be called great in the Kingdom of Heaven. For I tell you, that unless your righteousness exceeds that of the scribes and Pharisees, under no circumstances will you enter the Kingdom of Heaven. Nevertheless, it is impossible for man to obey all of G-d's commandments.

At this, one of the disciples asked him, "Then how can any man be justified in the sight of G-d?" To which Jesus replied:

Long before the Law was given, the LORD appeared to Abraham and proclaimed the "good news" then he would justify the Gentiles through faith. At that time, G-d said to Abraham, "In you shall all nations be blessed." He also said, "To your seed will I give this land." He did not say, 'To your seeds,' as though speaking of more than one; but he said, 'To your seed.' Wherefore, all those who live by faith are counted as the children of Abraham. If there would have been a law that could have given eternal life, then grace and mercy should have first appeared in the Law of Moses; but such was not the case. Indeed, the Law of the LORD is perfect and enlightens the eyes of the transgressors, for whom it was given. However, the Law does not annul the promises of G-d that were in effect before the Law came into being. Otherwise, how would Abraham be justified in the sight of G-d? The Scripture says that Abraham believed G-d; and because of his faith, grace was imputed to him. Remember this: When your fathers were first brought out of the land of Egypt, they were not given any commandments concerning burnt offerings and sacrifices. Instead, they were given this statute:"

If you will diligently listen to the voice of the LORD, your G-d, and will do that which is right in my eyes, then I will be your G-d, and you will be my people.

The LORD does not look at things the way man does. Man looks on the outward appearance; but the LORD looks on the heart. A man can refrain from all appearances of violating the commandments in his flesh, but in his heart he can be full of wickedness. Therefore, it is written in the Holy Scriptures, 'In the light of the Kings countenance there is life.' For it is not by works alone that one finds grace and mercy in the eyes of G-d, but by faith. For example, it was taught by them in the old days, 'You shall not commit murder,' and, 'Whosoever commits murder will be in danger of the judgment.' But, I tell you that whoever is angry with his brother without good reason is in danger of the judgment. Also, whoever will say to his brother, Raca, (worthless one) will be in danger of the council. But, the one who says to his brother, 'You fool,' is in danger of hell fire.

Therefore, when you have brought your gift to the altar, and remember that your brother has something against you; leave your gift at the altar and go to him. First be reconciled to your brother, then come and offer your gift. Agree with your adversary quickly, while you have the opportunity. Make peace before he brings you to the judge, and the judge delivers you to the officer to be cast into prison. Truly, I say to you, you won't be able to come out from there until you have paid the very last farthing.

You have heard that it was taught by them in the old days, 'You shall not commit adultery.' But I tell you that whoever looks on a woman lustfully has already broken the commandment, because he has committed adultery with her in his heart. If your right eye causes you to offend, pluck it out and cast it away. It is better for you that one of your members should perish, than to have your whole body cast into hell.

It has also been taught, 'Whoever wants to divorce his wife, let him give her a writ of divorce.' But I tell you this: whoever will divorce his wife, unless she is guilty of fornication, causes her to commit adultery; and whoever marries a divorced woman commits adultery.

Again, you have heard that this was taught by them in the old days: 'You shall not perjure yourself, but shall perform unto the LORD your oaths.' But I tell you not to swear at all. Don't swear by heaven, because it is G-d's throne; nor by the earth, because it is his footstool. Don't swear by Jerusalem either, because it's the City of the great King. Neither are you to swear by your head, because you can't make one hair white or black. Instead, let your answers be a simple yes, or no, for anything beyond this comes from the evil one.

You have heard them teach, 'An eye for an eye, and a tooth for a tooth.' But I say to you, don't oppose an evil person. If he strikes you on your right cheek, turn to him the other also. If he wants to sue you and take away your coat, let him have your cloak also. If someone forces you to go a mile with him; go two miles. Give to him that asks you, and from him who wishes to borrow from you, don't turn away.

You have heard it said, 'Love your neighbor and hate your enemies.' But I say to you: Love your enemies. Bless those who curse you. Do good to those that hate you. Pray for all who are spiteful toward you and oppress you; so that you may be the children of your Heavenly Father. For he makes the sun to shine on the evil as well as the good, and sends rain on both the just and the unjust. If you only love those who love you, what reward do you have? Don't even the public officials do the same thing? Therefore, you be perfect, as your Father in heaven is perfect.

Be careful not to perform your charitable acts before men, just to be seen by them. Otherwise, you will have no reward from your Heavenly Father. When you practice your works of charity, don't sound the trumpet in front of you like the hypocrites do. They flaunt themselves in the synagogues and in the streets, so that they may have the praises of men.

Truly, I say to you, they have received their reward. But you, when you perform your works of charity and righteousness, don't let your left hand know what your right hand is doing. Let your works be done in secret. Then your Father, who sees everything that is done in secret, will openly reward you himself.

When you pray, don't be like the hypocrites! They love to pray standing in the synagogues and on the street corners, so they can be seen of men. Truly, I tell you, they have their reward. But you, when you pray, go into your closet. When you have shut the door, pray to your Father in secret; and your Father who sees in secret will openly reward you. Also, when you are praying, do not use vain repetitions like the heathen do. They believe they will be heard if they speak a great many words. Don't be like them. Your Father knows what you are in need of before you ask. When you pray, pray after this manner:

> Our Father, who is in heaven praise be to your holy name. Let your kingdom, come; and let your will be done in the earth as it is in heaven. Give us day by day our daily bread; and forgive us our debts, as we forgive our debtors. Lead us away from temptation, and deliver us from evil. For the Kingdom, the power and the glory is yours forever. Amen.

If you forgive men their offenses, your Heavenly Father will also forgive you. But, if you will not forgive men their offenses, neither will your Heavenly Father forgive yours.

Don't be like the hypocrites when you are fasting either. They distort their faces and walk before men with a dreary and drained expression so that people will know they are fasting. Truly, I tell you, they have their reward. But when you fast, anoint your head and wash your face. This way you won't appear to be fasting to men, but only to your Heavenly Father, who will reward you openly.

Don't stockpile treasures upon the earth that can be destroyed by moths or rust, and where thieves can break in and steal them. Reserve for yourselves treasures in heaven, that cannot be corrupted by moths or rust, and where no thief can break in to steal. For where your treasure is, that is where your heart will be.

The light of the body is the eye. Therefore, if your eye is clear, your whole body will be full of light. But, if your eye is obscure, your whole body is full of darkness. If the light that is in you be obscured, how great that darkness is!

No man can serve two masters. He will either hate the one and love the other; or, he will hold on to the one and despise the other. You cannot serve G-d and wealth. Therefore, I say to you, don't be concerned about your life and worry about what you will eat or drink. Neither should you be concerned about your body and worry about what you will wear. Is your life not more important than the food you eat, and your body more important than the clothes you wear? Look at the birds! They neither plant, harvest, nor gather into barns; yet, your Heavenly Father feeds them. Don't you think you are more important than they are? Which of you, by worrying, can add one cubit to his height? Why worry about clothing? Consider the lilies of the field and how they grow. They don't labor, nor do they spin. Yet, I tell you that Solomon, in all of his glory, was not garnished like one of these. Now, if G-d clothes the grass of the field, which is here today, and cast into the fire tomorrow, will he not clothe you even more? O' you of little faith!

Therefore, don't concern yourself with what you will eat or drink, or, what you will wear. The pagans spend their time running after these things. Your Heavenly Father knows that you need them. Seek after the Kingdom of G-d, and his righteousness, and all these things will be given to you. Don't worry about tomorrow. Let tomorrow worry about itself. Each day has a sufficient amount of its own trouble.

Don't judge, or you will be judged too. For in the same manner that you judge others, you will be judged; and the same measure that you use, it will be measured back to you again. Besides, why look for the speck in your brother's eye and pay no attention to the beam that is in your own eye? Or, how can you say to your brother, 'Let me pull the speck out of your eye,' when you have a beam in your own? That is a hypocrite! First pull the beam out of your own eye, then you will be able to see clearly enough to pull the speck out of your brother's eye.

Don't give that which is sacred to the dogs; neither cast your pearls before the swine. Otherwise, they may trample them under their feet and turn back and tear you apart.

Ask, and it will be given to you. Seek, and you will find. Knock, and it will be opened to you. Everyone who asks receives; and everyone who searches finds what he is looking for. To him who knocks, the door will be opened. Remember how it is written in the Scriptures:

If you cry after knowledge, and pray for understanding; if you seek her as silver, and search for her as you would for a hidden treasure; then you will understand the fear of the LORD, and find the knowledge of G-d. For the LORD, himself, gives wisdom; and out of his mouth comes knowledge and discernment. Therefore, do not be wise in your own eyes. In all things acknowledge the LORD and he will direct your paths.

Which one of you men, if your son asks you for bread, will give him a stone? Or, if he asks for a fish, will hand him a serpent? If you then, being sinful, know how to give good things to your children, how much more will your Heavenly Father give good things to those that ask him? Therefore, in everything, do onto others what you would have them do to you, for this is the essence of the Law and the prophets.

Enter in at the narrow gate. The gate that leads to destruction is wide; and because the road is broad that leads to it, there will be a great many entering therein. But the gate is small and the road is narrow that leads to eternal life, and only a few will find it.

Watch out for false prophets. They come to you disguised in sheep's clothing, but inwardly they are hungry wolves. You will know them by their fruit. Do men gather grapes from thorn bushes, or figs from thistles? A good tree cannot bear bad fruit; neither can a bad tree bear good fruit. Every tree that does not bear good fruit is cut down and thrown into the fire. Therefore, by their fruit shall you know them.

Not everyone who cries out to me, 'LORD, LORD,' will enter into the Kingdom of Heaven; only he that does the will of my Father, who is in heaven. For many will say to me in that day, 'LORD, LORD, have we not prophesied in your name? In your name, have we not cast out devils and performed many miracles?' At that time, I will declare to them, I never knew you; depart from me all of you who work iniquity.

There are seven abominations that are detestable to the LORD: a proud look; a lying tongue; hands that shed innocent blood; a heart that devises wicked schemes; feet that are quick to rush into evil; a false witness; and a man who stirs up dissension between brothers; and they will not go unpunished. However, the man who refuses to walk in the counsel of the ungodly whose delight is in the word of G-d; even he obtains G-d's favor and receives the blessings of the LORD.

Therefore, whoever listens to my teachings, and does them, I will liken him to a wise man that built his house upon a rock. The rains came down, the waters rose, and the winds blew and beat against the house. Nonetheless, it did not fall because it was founded upon a rock. However, everyone that listens to my teachings and does not put them into practice, I will compare to a foolish man who built his house upon the sand. The rains came down, the waters rose, and the winds blew and beat against the house, and it collapsed with a mighty crash."

VII.

As Jesus stood by Lake Gennesaret, a leper came to him and prostrated himself saying, "LORD, if you will, you can make me clean." Moved with compassion, Jesus stretched out his hand and touched him saying, "I will; be clean." Immediately, the man was cured of his leprosy and his flesh became as the flesh of a little child. Then Jesus said to him, "See that you tell no one: but go your way, show yourself to the priest and offer the gift that Moses commanded in the Law for a testimony against them. Go in peace."

Turning around, Jesus saw two boats docked by the lake, but the fishermen were not in them because they had gone to wash their nets. He boarded the one that belonged to Simon and asked him to push out a little from the land. Then he sat down and taught the people from the ship, proclaiming the words of the Father saying:

> Hear, the word of our G-d, O' Israel, as it is written in the book of Moses: The LORD our G-d is one LORD! And you shall love the LORD your G-d with all your heart, and with all your soul, and with all your might. The LORD did not set his love upon you because you had the largest population among all the people of the earth; in fact, you had the smallest population. It was because the LORD loved this nation, and wished to fulfill his oath to Abraham that he brought your fathers out of the land of Egypt, and redeemed them out of the house of bondage.

Know and understand this: the LORD, our G-d, is the only true G-d; and he is a faithful G-d, who keeps his promises and his mercy with all those who love him and practice his commandments, even to a thousand generations. Hear this, all you people! Give me your attention, all of you who inhabit this land; both the lowly and the prominent, the rich and the poor together; for I will speak in the bitterness of my soul. The LORD has spoken, saying: I have nourished and brought up children, and they have rebelled against me. The ox knows his owner, and the donkey knows his master's stall; but Israel does not know, neither do my people even consider that they have forsaken the LORD, provoked the Holy One of Israel to anger and have gone backwards! The whole head is sick and the heart is weak. For this reason your country is desolate, your cities are burned to the ground and strangers devour the land in your presence. Here now my reasoning, and listen to my pleading. Wash yourselves, and make yourselves clean! Put away the evil from before my eyes. Learn righteousness by seeking justice: relieve the oppressed and plead the cause of the fatherless and the widows. Come, let us reason together. Though your sins are as scarlet, they will be made as white as snow. If you are willing and obedient, you will enjoy the goodness of the land; but, if you refuse and rebel, you will be devoured by the sword, for the mouth of the LORD has declared it. O' house of Jacob, come and let us walk in the light of the LORD! For those who are blessed by him will inherit the earth; but they that are cursed shall die.

Repent! Turn away from all your transgressions! Cast your sins away from you and prepare to make your heart clean and your spirit upright. The LORD will never turn away from such, but he is ever merciful to the sincere in heart. Therefore, turn back to the LORD, your G-d, and wait on him continually. For this is what the LORD has said: 'Turn to me with all your heart, with fasting, weeping and mourning; and rend your hearts rather than your garments.' Now, don't be stubborn and hardhearted, but surrender yourselves to the LORD. Enter into his sanctuary which he has sanctified forever; and serve the LORD, your G-d. If you turn back to the LORD, your brethren and your children will find compassion in the eyes of them that hold you captive. And, it will come to pass that whosoever will call upon the name of the LORD will be saved. For our G-d, alone, is the G-d of salvation.

Turning to his disciples, Jesus said, "Gather all the people together, both the adults and the youth, and baptize them." At that time many of the people came forward to be baptized and to enter into a covenant with the LORD to seek him and to serve him with all their heart and soul. When he had finished ministering to the people, Jesus said to Simon, "Launch out into the waters and let your nets down for a catch." Then Simon said to him, "Master, we have worked all night and have caught nothing!" Jesus gave him a 'knowing' look. "Nevertheless, at your word, I will let down the net." When they lowered the net they caught a great multitude of fish, so much so, that the net broke. Excitedly they summoned their partners who had launched out in the other ship to come and help them. Working feverishly, they filled both ships with so many fish they began to sink.

When Simon Peter saw the extent of it all, he fell down at Jesus' knees and said, "Leave me now, LORD; for I am such a sinful man." Then Jesus said, "Simon, don't be afraid; hereafter you will catch men." Peter was astonished, and so were all that were with him, including James and John, the sons of Zebedee, who were partners with Simon, when they witnessed the great number of fish they had caught. And after they brought their ships to shore, they forsook everything and followed him.

Later that day, Jesus separated himself from them and went into the wilderness to pray. Lifting up his eyes and hands toward heaven Jesus said: "Many, O' LORD my G-d, are the wonderful works which you have done! I delight in fulfilling your will, my G-d: yes, your Law is within my soul. I have preached your righteousness to the masses and have not withheld my lips from preaching. Neither did I hide your righteousness within my heart; for I have declared your faithfulness and your salvation. I will cause your name to be remembered throughout all future generations; so that the people will praise you forever and ever. Be exalted, O' G-d, above the heavens; and let your glory be above all the earth!

Make a joyful noise to G-d, all you lands! Sing forth the honor of his name and make his praises glorious! Let it be said of G-d, 'How fearful are you in all your works! Through the greatness of your power shall your enemies submit themselves to you!' For all the earth shall worship you, and will sing to you and to your name. Blessed be the LORD! Hallelujah!

One particular day, as Jesus was teaching, he was interrupted by the noise of a man breaking through the ceiling tiles. Some men had brought a man on a bier which had been afflicted with palsy. They tried to find a way to bring him into the house and to lay him before Jesus, but, when they could not get to the door because of the crowds, they went upon the house top and let him down through the tiling. When Jesus saw their faith, he said to the man, "Man, your sins are forgiven."

At that time there were Pharisees and doctors of the Law present which had come from Galilee, Judea and Jerusalem; and the power of the LORD was present to heal them all. When they heard these words, they began to reason within themselves, saying, "Who is this speaking blasphemies? Who can forgive sins, but G-d?" But when Jesus perceived their thoughts, he said to them, "What is this that you are pondering in your hearts? Which is easier to say, 'Your sins are forgiven,' or, 'Rise up and walk?' But this is said in order that you may know that the Son of Man has power on earth to forgive sins." (He said to the palsy victim) "I say to you, 'Arise, take up your couch and go to your house.'" Immediately he stood up before them all, took up his bed and departed to his house glorifying G-d. Filled with astonishment and fear, they said, "We have seen some very strange things today."

After these things Jesus went out and met a tax collector named Levi, (Matthew), and said to him," Follow me." Immediately, he left everything, stood up and followed him. Levi made a great feast and invited a great many public officials and common folk to his house. Then the scribes and Pharisees began to murmur to the followers of Jesus, "Why do you eat and drink with public officials and sinners?" "Those who are healthy don't need a physician," Jesus interjected, "only those who are sick. However, go and learn what this means, 'I want a show of mercy, not sacrifice.' I did not come to call the righteous, but the sinners to repentance." Then they said to him, "Why do the disciples of John and the Pharisees fast and pray often, but yours eat and drink?" In reply, Jesus said, "Can you make the guests of the bridegroom fast while he is with them? But the days will come when the bridegroom will be taken away from them; and then they will fast in those days."

Then he spoke a parable: "No one puts a patch from a new garment on an old one. If they do, the new garment is torn and the piece that was taken from it does not agree with the old. Nor does anyone put new wine into old wineskins. Otherwise, the new wine will cause the wineskins to burst, the wine to be spilled, and the skins to be ruined. New wine must be put into new wineskins in order for both to be preserved. Besides, no one having drunk old wine immediately desires the new, because he says the old wine is better."

Leaving that place, Jesus traveled to Jerusalem to celebrate a feast of the Jews. Near the Sheep Gate at Jerusalem, there was a pool which had five porches called Bethesda in the Hebrew tongue. In these were lodged a great number of disabled people; crippled, blind and paralyzed that sat there waiting for the water to move. For at a certain time an Angel would visit the pool and disturb the water; then whoever stepped into the water first would be healed of whatever disease he had. There was a certain man there who had been afflicted for some thirty-eight years. When Jesus saw him and knew that he had been in that condition for a long time, he said to the man, "Do you want to be made whole?" The invalid said, "Sir, I don't have anyone to put me into the pool after the water is disturbed. Instead, someone else always steps down before me." Then Jesus said to him, "Arise, pick up your bed and walk." Promptly, the man was made whole, and picked up his bed and walked. Now, this miracle was performed on the Sabbath day. Therefore, when the Jews saw him carrying his bed, they said to him, "Today is the Sabbath; it is unlawful for you to carry your bed!" The man replied, "The man who healed me told me to pick up my bed and walk." Then they asked him, "Who told you to pick up your bed and walk?" However, the man did not know who it was, for Jesus had slipped away from the multitude that was in that place.

Later on, Jesus found the man in the Temple and said to him, "Look, you are completely well! Now, don't sin anymore, lest something worse happens to you." When the man left the Temple, he told the Jews that it was Jesus who had healed him. Therefore, they persecuted him all the more and conspired to kill him because he had done these things on the Sabbath.

When Jesus said to them, "My Father is working here, and I am working", they desperately wanted to kill him not only because he had defiled the Sabbath, but also because he said that G-d was his Father making himself equal with G-d. Then Jesus delivered this message to them:

> I tell you the truth, the Son cannot do anything of his own mind. He can only do that which he sees the Father do: for the Son can do everything the Father does. Because the Father loves the Son, he shows him

everything that he does: and he will show him greater works than these that you may marvel. As the Father raises the dead and gives them life, even so the Son gives life to whomsoever he wishes.

The Father does not judge any man, but has committed all judgment to the Son; so that all men would honor the Son, even as they honor the Father. He that does not honor the Son does not honor the Father who sent him. Most assuredly I say to you, he that hears my words and believes on him that sent me, has everlasting life. He will not come into condemnation; but is crossed over from death to life. Truly, I tell you, the time is coming, and is already here, when the dead will hear the voice of the Son of G-d; and those who listen will live.

For as the Father has life in himself; so also has he granted the Son to have life in himself. He has also given him the authority to execute judgment because he is the Son of Man. Do not marvel at this: for the time is coming in which all that are in the graves will hear his voice and come out; they who have done good, to the resurrection of life; and they that have done evil, to the resurrection of the damned.

I can do nothing of my own mind: as I hear, I judge: and my judgment is just. Why? Because I do not seek my own will, but the will of the Father who sent me. If I bring glory to myself, my witness is not true. There is another that bears witness of me; and I know that his witness of me is true.

You sent for John, and he testified of the truth. But I do not receive testimony from any man: I say these things to you so that you might be saved. He was a burning and shining light: and you were willing for a time to rejoice in his light. But I have a weightier testimony than John; for the works which the Father has given me to finish, they are the works which testify that the Father has sent me. Even the Father himself, bears witness of me, whose voice you have not heard at any time, nor have you seen his shape. You do not have his word abiding in you either; for you do not believe the one whom he has sent. Search the Scriptures: for in them you think you have eternal life: but they are the same words that testify of me. Yet, you will not come to me so that you might live.

I don't receive honor from man. But, I know that you don't have the love of G-d in you. I have come in my Father's name and you do not accept me; but if someone else comes in their own name, you will receive him. How can you believe when you accept praise from one another, yet make no effort to seek the praise that comes from G-d alone? Don't think that I will make an accusation against you to my Father. There is another that accuses you, even Moses in whom you trust. For if you had believed Moses, you would have believed me, because he wrote about me. But, if you don't believe his writings, how will you believe my words? How well did Jeremiah prophesy of you when he said:

To whom shall I speak and give a warning, that they may hear? Behold, their ear is uncircumcised, and they cannot listen. The word of the LORD is despised by them; they have no delight in it. For from the least of them to the greatest, every one of them is given to greed.

The following Sabbath Jesus and his disciples were walking through the cornfield when his disciples were observed plucking ears of corn and eating them. Then certain Pharisees confronted them and asked, "Why do you do those things that are unlawful on the Sabbath day?" Before they could give an answer, Jesus said, "Have you never read what David did when he, and his men were hungry? How he went into the house of G-d, took and ate the consecrated bread, and gave some to the men that were with him; which is not lawful for any man to eat except for the priests alone? Or, have you never read in the Law how, on the Sabbath days, the priests in the Temple profane the Sabbath and are blameless? I tell you that there is one standing here who is greater than the Temple. But, if you would have learned what this means, 'I want mercy not sacrifice,' you would not have condemned the innocent. For the Son of Man is LORD, even of the Sabbath day."

On another Sabbath Jesus entered the synagogue to teach, and there was a man present whose hand was crippled. The scribes and Pharisees watched him closely to see whether or not he would heal on the Sabbath day, so they might accuse him. Finally, they asked him, "Is it lawful to heal on the Sabbath day?" But, knowing their thoughts, he said to the man with the crippled hand, "Rise up, and stand here in the midst of us"; and the man stood up and went forward. Then Jesus addressed the leaders of the synagogue, "I will ask you; is it lawful on the Sabbath days to do good, or evil;

to save life, or destroy it? Which one of you will have one lamb, and if it falls into a pit on the Sabbath day, will not get a grasp on it and lift it out?" When none of them answered, he said, "How much better is a man than a sheep than? Therefore, it must be lawful to do good on the Sabbath days." After looking all around at each one of them, he said to the man, "Stretch out your hand." When he stretched it out, it was made whole like the other. The Jews were immediately consumed with anger and conspired with one another as to what they might do to Jesus.

In those days, Jesus went up into a mountain where he remained all night in prayer. When the morning came, he called his disciples together and selected twelve of them, whom he called apostles. He chose Simon, whom he surnamed Peter; Andrew, his brother; James and John, the sons of Zebedee; Philip, Matthew, Bartholomew (Nathaniel), Thomas, James, the son of Alphaeus; Simon, also called Zelotes; Judas, the brother of James; and Judas Iscariot, the one who would betray him.

When he came down from the mountain with his disciples, he found a multitude of people gathered together, waiting to hear his teachings and to be cured of their diseases. Many were from Judea and Jerusalem, but some had come from as far away as Tyre and Sidon. They were all trying to touch him because virtue came out from him and healed them all, including those who had been vexed with unclean spirits. Then he began to teach them, saying:

Blessed are you poor, for the Kingdom of Heaven is yours. Blessed are you that are hungry now, because you will be filled. Blessed are you that weep now, for you will laugh. You are blessed when others hate you and separate you from their company; insult you and bring disgrace upon your name for my name's sake. Rejoice in that day and jump for joy; because your reward is great in heaven. Their ancestors did the same thing to the prophets.

Woe unto you who are rich! Surely, you have received your consolation! Woe to you whose bellies are full; for you will be hungry! Woe unto you who laugh now; for you will weep and mourn! Woe unto you when others speak kindly of you; for their forefathers did the same thing to the false prophets!

To those of you who are listening to what I am saying: I am telling you to love your enemies, and to do good things for those who hate you. Bless those who curse you; and pray for the ones who mistreat you. To him who would strike you on the one cheek, offer him the other also. If someone takes away your cloak, don't forbid him to take away your coat also. Give to everyone who asks something of you; and as for the one who steals your goods, don't ask him to return them. As you would like for others to treat you, treat them the same way. If you only love those who love you, what thanks do you have? For even the unbelievers love those who love them in return! If you only do good to those who can return the kindness, what credit is that to you? Even the unbelievers do that much! Also, if you only lend to those who are able to repay you, what credit is that to you? Even the unbelievers lend to one another because they hope to be repaid in full! If you will love your enemies, doing good to them, and lend, hoping for nothing in return, your reward will be great; and you will be called the children of the Most High; because G-d is kind even to the ungrateful and the wicked. Therefore, be merciful; just as your Father is merciful.

Don't judge others, and you will not be judged. Don't condemn others, and you will not be condemned. Forgive, and you will be forgiven. Give, and it will be returned to you; good measure, pressed down, shaken together and running over will men give into your bosom. For with the same measure that you measure with, it will be measured back to you again.

Can the blind lead the blind? Will they both not fall into the ditch? The student is not above his teacher: but everyone that has been perfected will be like his teacher. Why do you look for the speck that is in your brother's eye, but can't perceive the beam that is in your own eye? You are being a hypocrite! First, cast out the beam that is in your own eye, and then you will see clearly enough to pull the speck out of your brother's eye.

A good tree cannot bear corrupt fruit; neither does a corrupt tree bear good fruit. Every tree can be recognized by the fruit it produces. Men don't gather figs from thorn bushes; neither do they gather grapes from briars. A good man, out of the good treasure in his heart, brings forth teachings that are good; and an evil man, out of the evil treasure in his heart, brings to the surface teachings that are evil because he draws out his words from the resources retained in his heart.

Why do you call out to me, 'LORD, LORD,' and don't do the things I say? Whosoever comes to me, listens to my teachings and puts them into practice; I will show you whom he is like. He is like a man who built a house, and having dug deep into the ground, laid the foundation on a rock. When the flood arose and the stream beat against the house violently, it couldn't shake it because it was built on a rock. However, the one who listens to my words and does not put them into practice is like another man who built a house upon the ground, without a foundation. When the stream beat violently against it, it fell immediately; and the destruction of that house was massive.

When Jesus had concluded his message to the people, he entered the city of Capernaum where he was soon approached by several elders of the people. They had been sent by a certain centurion to urge Jesus to come and heal one of his servants who was very sick and near death. When they found Jesus, they immediately began to plead with him, telling him that the centurion was worthy of his mercy because he loved their nation and was instrumental in building them a new synagogue. Then Jesus went with them. As he neared the house, the centurion sent some friends to him with this message, "LORD, don't trouble yourself: for I am not worthy that you should enter under my roof; neither did I think that I was worthy to come to you; but say the word, and my servant will be healed. For I, too, am a man in a position of authority, having many soldiers under me; if I say to one, 'go,' he goes. If I say to another, 'come,' he comes; and if I say to my servant, 'do this,' he does it." When Jesus heard these words, he marveled; and turning around to the people that followed him, he said, "I tell you, I have not found such great faith in all of Israel! Furthermore, I will tell you this: many will come from the east and the west and will sit down with Abraham, Isaac, and Jacob in the Kingdom of Heaven, but the children of the Kingdom will be cast out into utter darkness, where there will be weeping and gnashing of teeth." Then he turned back to the friends of the centurion and said, "Go your way; and give your friend this message, 'As you have believed, so be it done to you.'" When they returned to the house, they found the servant well that had been sick.

The following day he went to a village called Nain; and many of his disciples went with him. As he approached the entrance of the village, he observed a mourning processional. The dead man being carried out was the only son of his widowed mother. When the LORD saw the bereaved mother, he had compassion on her and said, "Don't cry." He walked over and touched the bier, and the pall bearers stood still. Then he said to the dead man, "Young man, I say to you, arise." Immediately, the young man sat up and began to speak; and Jesus brought him to his mother. A great fear fell upon the multitude, and they glorified G-d, saying that a great prophet had risen from among them, and that G-d had visited his people. Their testimony of him continued to spread throughout Judea and all the surrounding regions.

When John heard these things concerning Jesus, he sent two of his disciples to him saying, "Are you the one that is supposed to come, or do we look for another?" In that same hour, Jesus cured many of their infirmities and diseases, delivered scores from evil spirits, and brought sight to the blind. Then Jesus turned to the disciples of John and said, "Go and tell John the things that you have seen and heard; how the blind see, the lame walk, the lepers are cleansed, the deaf hear, the dead are raised, and the gospel is preached to the poor. Tell him, 'Blessed is he that is not offended in me.'"

When the messengers of John departed, he began to speak to the people concerning John, saying, "What did you go out into the desert to see, a reed shaken with the wind? What did you go out expecting to see a man clothed in delicate clothes? Observe for yourselves; those who are dressed beautifully and live delicately reside in king's courts. So what did you go out expecting to see, a prophet? Yes; and I tell you, much more than a prophet. This is he, of whom it is written, 'Behold I send my messenger before your face which shall prepare the way before you.' I tell you, among those who are born of women, there is no greater prophet than John, the Baptist. Notwithstanding, he that is least in the Kingdom of G-d is greater than he. From the days of John, the Baptist, until now, the Kingdom of Heaven suffers violence, and the violent take it by force. For all the prophets and the Law prophesied until John, and, if you will accept it, this is Elijah, who was supposed to come. He that has ears to hear, let him pay attention."

All the people that heard him, including the public officials, justified G-d because they had been baptized by John. But the Pharisees and lawyers rejected the counsel of G-d against themselves, for they had not been baptized by him. Then the LORD said to them, "To whom shall I compare the men of this age; what are they like? They are like children sitting in the marketplace and calling out to each other: 'We have played music for you, and you did not dance; we have mourned for you, but you did not cry.' For John the Baptist came to you, neither eating bread nor drinking wine, and you said he has a devil. "The Son of Man has come to you, both eating and drinking, and you say, 'Look at this gluttonous drunk, the friend of public officials and sinners!' But, wisdom is justified by all of her children." Then he began to denounce the cities in which most of his miraculous works were done, because they didn't repent:

Woe be to you, Chorazin! Woe to you Bethsaida! For if the miracles which were performed in you had been done in Tyre and Sidon, they would have repented long ago in sackcloth and ashes! I say to you, it will be more tolerable for Tyre and Sidon at the day of judgment than for you! And you, Capernaum, who thinks you will be exalted up to heaven, you will be brought down to hell! For if the miracles which were performed in you had been done in Sodom, it would have remained until this day! But, I tell you, it will be more tolerable for the land of Sodom in the day of judgment than for you!

I thank you, O' Father, LORD of heaven and earth, because you have hidden these things from the wise and prudent and have revealed them to babes. Even so, Father, because it was pleasing in your sight.

(Turning back to the people, Jesus continued his message).

All things have been committed to me from my Father. No one knows the Son except the Father; Neither does anyone know the Father, except the Son and, whomever the Son will reveal him to. Come to me, all of you that are weary and heavily burdened, and I will give you rest. Take my yoke upon yourself and learn about me; for I am meek and humble in heart, and you will find rest for your souls. My yoke is easy, and my burden is light.

One of the Pharisees asked him if he would come and dine with him; wherefore, Jesus accompanied him to his house and reclined at the table. When a certain woman in the city, who had lived a sinful life, discovered that Jesus was dining at the Pharisees' house, she took an alabaster box of ointment and stood behind him crying. She knelt down and began to wash his feet with her tears and to wipe them with the hairs of her head. Then, kissing his feet, she anointed them with the ointment. When the Pharisee saw this, he spoke within his heart, "If this man was a prophet, he would know who was touching him and what kind of sinful woman she is." Knowing his thoughts, Jesus said to him, "Simon, I have something to say to you." He answered, "Speak, Rabbi." Then Jesus said, "There were two men who owed a certain creditor some money: one owed five hundred pence, and the other fifty. When they didn't have the money to pay, he frankly forgave them both. Tell me, which one of them will love him the most?" Simon answered, "I suppose the one who had the larger debt canceled." Looking at the woman Jesus said, "You have judged correctly. Do you see this woman? When I entered your house, you gave me no water for my feet; but she has washed my feet with tears and wiped them with the hairs of her head. You gave me no kiss: but since I came in, this woman has not stopped kissing my feet. You didn't anoint my head with oil; but this woman has anointed my feet with ointment. Therefore, I tell you this - her sins which are many, are forgiven because she has loved much; but to whom little is forgiven, the same loves little." Then Jesus said to the woman, "Your sins are forgiven. Your faith has saved you; go in peace." Then those who were dining with him began to say within themselves, "Who is this that forgives sins?" After this Jesus and his disciples went throughout every city and village preaching and showing the glad tidings of the kingdom of G-d.

Among his disciples were several women who had been healed of evil spirits and infirmities, namely: Mary, called Magdalene, out of whom went seven devils; and Joanna, the wife of Chuza, Herod's steward; as well as many others which ministered to him out of their own substance. A great multitude followed him, and he healed them all. And in him was the prophecy of Isaiah fulfilled:

Behold my servant whom I have chosen; my beloved in whom my soul delights. I will put my Spirit upon him and he will show judgment to the Gentiles. He will not argue, nor cry out; no one will hear his voice in the streets. A bruised reed will he not break, and a smoldering wick will he not snuff out until he leads justice to victory. In his name shall the Gentiles trust.

Then they brought a demon possessed man who was both blind and dumb; and Jesus healed him, so that he could both see and speak. When the people saw this miracle, they were astonished and said, "Could this be the Son of David?" But when the Pharisees heard this, they thought within themselves, "This fellow doesn't cast out devils except through Beelzebub, the Prince of the devils." Knowing their thoughts, Jesus said to them:

Every kingdom divided against itself is brought to desolation; and every city or house divided against itself will not stand. Now, if Satan casts himself out, and he is divided against himself, how can his kingdom stand? And, if I cast out devils by Beelzebub, by whom do your children cast them out? Let them be your judges. But, if I cast out devils by the Spirit of G-d, then the Kingdom of G-d has come to you. Besides, how can one enter a strong man's house and steal his goods unless he first ties up the strong man? Then he is able to rob his house.

He that is not with me is against me; and the one who doesn't gather with me scatters abroad. Therefore, I say to you that all manner of sin and blasphemy will be forgiven men, but blasphemy against the Holy Ghost will never be forgiven. Whoever speaks a word against the Son of Man will be forgiven: but, whoever speaks a word against the Holy Ghost will never be forgiven, not in this world, nor in the world to come. Either make the tree and its fruit good; or else, make the tree and its fruit corrupt; for the tree is known by its fruit.

O' generation of vipers, how can you, being evil, teach good things? For out of the abundance of information stored in the heart, the mouth speaks. A good man brings forth good teachings out of the good stored within him; and an evil man brings forth evil teachings out of the evil stored up within him. Wherefore, I tell you that men will have to give an account of every idle word that they have spoken in the day of judgment. By your words will you be justified or condemned.

VIIII.

Several of the scribes and Pharisees came to Jesus privately and said, "Teacher, we want to see you perform a miracle." But he answered them by saying:

An evil and adulterous generation looks for miracles and signs! But, no sign will be given to it except the sign of the prophet Jonah; for as Jonah spent three days and three nights in the fish's belly, so also shall the Son of Man spend three days and nights in the heart of the earth.

The men of Nineveh will rise up at the judgment against this generation and condemn it, because they repented at the preaching of Jonah; and look, one greater than Jonah is here. The queen of the south will rise up at the judgment against this generation and condemn it, because she came from the ends of the earth to hear the wisdom of Solomon; and look, one greater than Solomon is here.

When the unclean spirit goes out of a man, it walks through dry places, looking for rest; and unable to find it, the spirit says, 'I will return to the house I left.' Then, when it reenters the house and finds it empty, swept and set in order, it goes out and returns with seven other spirits more wicked than itself; and they enter him and live there. The final condition of that man is worse than at the beginning. That is how it will be with this wicked generation.

While he was speaking to the people, his mother and brothers stood on the outer perimeter of the crowd desiring to speak with him. Finally, someone said to him, "Look, your mother and your brothers are here, and they wish to speak to you." He said, "Who is my mother; and who are my brothers?" Then he stretched out his hand toward his followers and said, "Behold, my mother and my brothers! For whoever will perform the will of my Father, who is in heaven, the same is my brother, sister and mother."

That same day, Jesus went out and sat by the seaside. Because the crowds that had gathered were so great, he entered a boat, and taught the people from there in the form of parables:

A certain farmer went out to plant his seed. As he scattered the seed, some of it fell by the wayside, and the fowls came and devoured them. Some fell in rocky places where there was very little soil, and they sprung up rapidly. When the sun came up, the plants were scorched and withered away quickly, because they had no roots. Some others fell among thorns; and the thorns grew up and choked them. But, others fell onto good ground and produced a crop; some a hundred times, some sixty times, and some thirty times more than what was sown. Whoever has ears to hear, let him pay close attention.

Then his disciples asked him, "Why do you speak to them in parables?" Jesus replied:

Because it is intended for you to know the secrets of the Kingdom of Heaven. Therefore, they are given to you, not to them. Whoever has will be given more, and he will have an abundance; but whoever is lacking, even what little he has will be taken away from him. I speak to them in parables because they think they see; they think they are hearing, and they believe that they understand; but they neither see, hear, nor understand. In them is the prophecy of Isaiah fulfilled:

> *You will be ever hearing, but never understanding; you will be ever seeing, but never perceiving. For the hearts of these people have become calloused; they can barely hear with their ears, and they have closed their eyes; lest it come to pass that they might see with their eyes, hear with their ears, understand with their hearts, and be converted, so that I can heal them.*

But your eyes and ears are blessed, because they can both see and hear. Truly, I tell you that many prophets and righteous men have desired to see those things that you see, and to hear those things which you hear, and have not. Therefore, understand the parable of the farmer: when anyone hears the Word of the Kingdom and does not understand it, the devil comes and takes away that which was planted in his heart, lest they should believe and be saved. This is the one who received seed by the wayside. He that received seed in the stony places, the same is he that receives the Word with great joy; yet he has no confidence in himself. He endures for a while, but when persecution or tribulation arises because of the Word, he is offended and falls away. The one who received seed among the thorns is he that hears the Word, but the cares of this world and the deceitfulness of riches choke the Word, and he becomes unfruitful. But, he that received the seed on good soil is he, which in an honest and good heart, hears the Word, understands it, practices it, and brings forth fruit with patience. Some produce a hundred times more than what was sown; some produce sixty times more, and others produce thirty times more.

No man lights a candle and covers it with a lid, or puts it under a bed. Instead, he puts it on a candlestick so that all who enter may have light. For nothing is secret that will not be manifested; nor is anything hidden that will not be revealed. Therefore, be careful about what you listen to. For whoever has understanding, to him will be given more understanding; and whoever is without understanding, from him will be taken away even that which he thinks he has.

The Kingdom of Heaven is compared to a man who planted good seed in his field. While the servants slept, his enemy came and planted darnels among the wheat, and slipped away. When the wheat sprouted and produced fruit, then the darnels were plainly seen. So, the owner's servants went to him and said, 'Sir, did you not plant good seed in your field? Where did the darnels come from?' The owner said, 'An enemy of mine has done this.' Then his servants asked him, 'Do you want us to go and gather them up?' He said, 'No; because while you are pulling up the darnels, you may also uproot the wheat. Let them both grow up together until the harvest. At that time, I will say to the reapers, first gather the darnels into bundles to be burned, and then gather the wheat and bring it into my barn.'

The Kingdom of Heaven is likened to a grain of mustard seed, which a man took and planted in his field. Though it is the smallest of all the seeds, when it is grown, it is the largest of the herbs and becomes a tree, so that the birds of the air come and lodge in its branches. The Kingdom of Heaven is also compared to yeast, which a woman put in a large amount of flour until it worked all through the dough.

All these things Jesus taught the people in parables; and he never spoke to them without using a parable. Thus the prophecy of David was fulfilled: *I will open my mouth in parables; I will speak of things that have been kept a secret from the foundation of the world.*

After this, Jesus dismissed the multitudes and went into the house. Then his disciples sat down with him and said, "Explain to us the parable of the darnels." Jesus said to them:

He that plants the good seed is the Son of Man; the field is the world; the good seed are the children of the Kingdom; the darnels are the children of the wicked one; the enemy that planted them is the devil; the harvest is the end of the world; and the reapers are the Angels. Therefore, as the darnels are gathered and burned in the fire, so shall it be in the end of the world. The Son of Man will send forth his angels, who will gather out of his Kingdom everything that is offensive, and all those who commit iniquity, and will cast them into a furnace of fire, where there will be wailing and gnashing of teeth. Then the righteous will shine forth like the sun in the kingdom of his Father. Whoever has ears to hear, let him pay attention.

Again, the Kingdom of Heaven is compared to hidden treasure in a field, which a man hides after he has discovered it; and in his joy he goes and sells all that he has and buys that field.

The Kingdom of Heaven is also likened to a merchant seeking expensive pearls; who, when he found a pearl of great value, went and sold all that he had and bought it.

The Kingdom of Heaven is also compared to a net that was cast into the sea and caught all kinds of fish. When it was full, they drew it to shore, sat down, and separated the good from the bad. They put the good fish into baskets and cast the bad away. So shall it be at the end of the world. The Angels will come and separate the wicked from the just and cast them into a furnace of fire, where there will be weeping and gnashing of teeth.

"Have you understood all these things?" "Yes, LORD." They replied. Then he said, "Therefore, every teacher of the Law that is instructed in the Kingdom of Heaven is like the owner of the house who brings out of his treasure chest both new and old treasure."

One day Jesus entered a boat with his disciples and said to them, "Let's go to the other side of the lake." As they sailed, he fell asleep. Suddenly, a gusty wind storm arose over the lake: an event foretold in the book of Jonah:

> The LORD sent a great wind into the sea, a mighty tempest, so that the ship threatened to break up. But, he had gone below deck, where he lay down and fell asleep.

Finding themselves in jeopardy of sinking, they went to Jesus and aroused him, saying, "Master, Master, we are about to perish!" He arose from his sleep and rebuked the wind and the raging waters. Almost immediately there was a calm over the lake. Then he said to them, "Where is your faith?" Fearful, and completely overwhelmed by what they had just witnessed, they said to one another, "What kind of man is this? He even commands the winds and the water, and they obey him!" Thus another Scripture was fulfilled:

> They that go down to the sea in ships, that do their business in the great waters: these saw the works of the LORD, and his wonders in the deep; for he commanded, and raised a stormy wind, which lifted up the waves thereof. They mounted up to heaven, they went down to the depths. Their soul melted away because of trouble. They reeled back and forth, and staggered like drunkards, and are at their wits end. They cried to the LORD in their trouble, and he brought them out of their distresses. He made the storm a calm, so that the waves thereof were still. Then they were glad because they were quiet, and he led them to their desired haven.

They continued to sail to the region of the Gergesenes which is across the lake from Galilee. As soon as he stepped onto the land, he was met by a man from that region who was possessed with many devils. When the man saw him, he began to cry out in a loud voice, "What do you want with me, Jesus, Son of the Most High G-d? I beg you, please don't torment me!" For Jesus had commanded the unclean spirit to come out of the man. Many times in the past, the unclean spirits seized control of him. Although they chained him hand and foot in irons, he broke the chains and was driven by the demons into the wilderness, where he lived among the tombs. Jesus asked him, "What is your name?" "Legion," he replied, because many devils had entered into him. Then they begged him not to command them to return to the abyss. Nearby, a large herd of swine were feeding themselves on the hillside, and the demons pleaded with him to allow them to enter the swine. "Go," Jesus said. Immediately, the devils left the man and entered the swine, causing them to run wildly down the hill and into the lake where they drowned. When those tending the swine saw what happened, they ran to the city and told the story to the citizens, both of that city, and the surrounding countryside. Then they went out to see for themselves what had happened. When they came to Jesus and saw the man who had been possessed with devils sitting at his feet, fully clothed, and in his right mind, they were afraid. Those who had seen it began to tell them how the demoniac was cured. Overcome by fear, the Gergesenes asked Jesus to leave their country; and he returned to the boat and left. Now the man, out of whom the devils had departed, asked Jesus to permit him to accompany him. But, Jesus sent him away saying, "Return to your home and tell them how much G-d has done for you." So the man went his way and proclaimed all over town the wonderful things Jesus had done for him. Therefore, the next time Jesus returned, a large crowd welcomed him with great eagerness and expectation.

At that time a man named Jairus, a leader of the synagogue, came to Jesus and fell at his feet, urging him to come to his house. Jairus had a twelve-year-old daughter, his only child, and she was dying. As Jesus continued on his way, the crowds pressed hard against him. A certain woman who had a bleeding condition for twelve years, and who had spent all her money on physicians that could not heal her, came up behind him and touched the hem of his garment and her bleeding stopped immediately. "Who touched me?" Jesus asked. When they all denied it, Peter said to him, "Master, the people are pressing against you and crowding you, and you want to know who touched you?" "Someone touched me," Jesus said, "for I perceive that virtue has gone out from me." When Jesus gazed upon the woman, and she saw that she could not hide it from him, she came forward and fell down at his feet trembling with fear. Then in the presence of all the people, the woman told him why she had touched him and that she had been healed of her ailment. Moved with compassion, Jesus said, "Daughter, be comforted; your faith has healed you. Go in peace."

While he was speaking to the woman a messenger came from Jairus' house and said, "Don't trouble the teacher; your daughter is dead." When Jesus heard the report, he said to Jairus, "Don't be afraid: just believe and she will be healed." After he arrived at the house, he only permitted Peter, James, John, and the parents of the child to go in with him. As he entered the room, and found all who were present weeping and mourning for the girl, Jesus said to the crowd, "Stop crying, she isn't dead, she is only sleeping." They began to laugh at him and scorned him because they knew she was dead. After he escorted them all out of the room he went over to the girl, took her by the hand, and said, "Child, arise." At once, her spirit returned to her and she arose and stood upon her feet. Turning to the astonished parents, Jesus told them to give her something to eat, and ordered them not to tell anyone what was done.

Calling his twelve disciples together, he gave them power and authority to cast out devils and to cure all types of sickness and disease. Then he sent them out to preach the Kingdom of G-d with these instructions:

> Don't go among the Gentiles, nor enter into any of the houses of the Samaritans; for you are only being sent to the lost sheep of the family of Israel. As you go, preach; tell them that the Kingdom of G-d is near. Heal the sick, cleanse the lepers, raise the dead and cast out devils. You have freely received; therefore, freely give. Don't take along any gold, silver, nor brass in your belts. Don't take any script for your journey; neither carry an extra coat, pair of sandals, or a staff; for the worker is worthy of his keep. Whatever city or town you enter, search therein for someone who is credible, and abide there until you leave that place. When you enter the house, pronounce peace to it. If the house is worthy, let your peace remain; but if it is not worthy, let your peace return to you. Whosoever will not receive you, or listen to your words, shake the dust off your feet when you leave that house. Truly, I tell you, it will be more tolerable in the day of judgment for Sodom and Gomorrah than for that city.

> Listen to me; I am sending you out as sheep in the midst of wolves; therefore, be wise as serpents, and innocent as a dove. Ever be on your guard; for men will hand you over to their councils, and flog you in their synagogues. On account of me, you will be dragged before governors and Kings for a witness against them and the Gentiles. When they arrest you, don't worry about what to say or how to say it; for at that time it will be revealed to you what to say. For it

will not be you that is speaking, but the Spirit of your Father that will speak through you.

A brother will offer his own brother up to be killed; and a father his own child. Children will rebel against their parents and cause them to be put to death; and you will be hated by everyone for my name's sake; but the one who can endure to the end will be saved. When you are persecuted in one city, flee to another. For I am telling you the truth, you will not finish going through the cities of Israel before the Son of Man comes. The student is not greater than his teacher, neither is the servant above his master. If they have called the head of the house, Beelzebub, how many more things will they call the members of his household? Don't be afraid of them; for there is nothing concealed that will not be revealed, or hidden that will not be disclosed. What I tell you in the dark, speak in the daylight; and whatever is whispered in your ears, preach from the rooftops.

Do not be afraid of those who can only kill the body, but are unable to kill the soul. Instead, be afraid of him who can destroy both your body and soul in hell. Are two sparrows not sold for a penny? Yet, I tell you that not one of them falls to the ground without the consent of your Father. Even the very hairs of your head are numbered. Therefore, don't be afraid; you are more valuable than many sparrows. Whoever confesses me before men, I will also confess him before my Father in heaven. But whoever disavows me before men, I will also disavow him before my Father in heaven.

Do not think that I have come to bring peace upon the earth: I did not come to bring peace, but a sword. For I have come to turn a man against his father, the daughter against her mother, and the daughter-in-law against her mother-in-law; and a man's enemies will be those of his own household.

He that loves his father or mother more than me is not worthy of me: and he that loves his son or daughter more than me is not worthy of me. Furthermore, he that does not take up his cross and follow after me is not worthy of me. He that finds his life will lose it; and he that loses his life for my sake will find it. He that receives you, receives me; and he that receives me, receives him who sent me. He that receives a prophet because he is a prophet receives a prophet's reward; and he that receives a righteous man because he is righteous receives a righteous man's reward. And whoever will give a cup of cold water to one of these little ones, only in the name of a disciple, truly, I tell you with all certainty that he will never lose his reward.

IX.

When Herod, the tetrarch, heard the reports concerning Jesus, he said, "I have beheaded John; now who is this that I am hearing about?" Not many days before, Herod had John arrested and cast into prison for the sake of Herodias, his brother Philip's wife, because John had said to him, "It is not lawful for you to have her." Therefore, Herod desperately wanted to kill him; but he was afraid of the people because they considered John a prophet. At Herod's birthday party, the daughter of Herodias danced before them and she pleased Herod so much that he promised, with an oath, to give her whatever she asked for. Having been prompted by her mother in advance, she said, "Give me the head of John the Baptist here on a platter." Herod was greatly distressed by the request, but because he had sworn with an oath in front of his friends, he commanded that her request be carried out. After John was beheaded, they put his head on a platter and gave it to the girl, who quickly turned it over to her mother. When John's disciples heard what happened, they went to Herod and claimed his body; and after burying it, they found Jesus and told him that John was dead. Upon hearing the news about John, Jesus entered a boat and withdrew to a secluded place in the mountain with his disciples.

As soon as the people realized that he had left, they followed after him on foot from every town. When Jesus saw the crowds coming to him, he said to Philip, "Where can we buy bread for these people to eat?" He said this to prove

Philip, because he already knew what he was going to do. Philip answered, "Two hundred denarii worth of bread would not be enough for every one of them to take a little bite!" Then Andrew, Simon Peter's brother said, "There is a lad here who has five barley loaves and two small fish; but what is that among so many people?" Jesus said to him, "Bring them here to me." Now, there were about five thousand men, not counting women and children. After they brought the bread and fish to him, he said to his disciples, "Have the people sit down in groups of fifty."

When everyone was set, Jesus took the five loaves and the two fish, gave thanks and blessed them. Then he gave them to his disciples to distribute to the people and told them to give the people as much as they wanted. After they had eaten, he said to his disciples, "Gather up the fragments that remain so that nothing is wasted." When they discovered that they had filled twelve baskets with the leftovers, they were thoroughly amazed. The news of this great miracle spread quickly among the people and when they realized what Jesus had done, they said, "Without a doubt this is the prophet that is supposed to come into the world and save us from our enemies!" Therefore, when Jesus perceived that they wanted to take him by force and make him their King, he compelled his disciples to get into a ship and to go ahead of him to the other side while he dismissed the multitude. After he sent the multitudes away, he went up into the mountain to pray alone.

Later that evening, as the disciples were sailing across the sea toward Capernaum, the sea became rough and choppy because of a strong wind that had settled over the waters. Then, in the fourth watch of the night, Jesus went out to meet them, walking on the water. When the disciples saw him, they were terrified and cried out in fear, "It's a ghost!" Seeing their fright, Jesus called out to them, "Cheer up! It is I; don't be afraid." Then Peter said to him, "LORD, if it is really you, let me come to you on the water." "Come," Jesus said. Immediately, Peter climbed out of the boat and walked on the water toward him. However, when he saw the Tempest, he became afraid and began to sink. "LORD, save me!" He cried. At once, Jesus stretched out his hand, caught him, and said, "O' you of little faith! Why did you doubt?" After they climbed into the boat, the wind ceased. Then his disciples worshiped him, saying, "Truly, you are the Son of G-d!"

The next day, the crowd that had remained on the other side of the sea, unable to locate Jesus, began to reason among themselves. They took note that there had only been one boat there the day before, and that Jesus' disciples had left in it while leaving him behind. (However, other boats had come from Tiberias and landed nearby since then). Nevertheless, when they realized that neither Jesus, nor his disciples were there, they also entered boats and went to Capernaum looking for him. When they found him, they said, "Rabbi, when did you get here?" Jesus answered, "Truly, I tell you, you didn't look for me because you saw the miracles, but because you ate from the loaves and were filled. Don't work for the food that spoils, but for the food that endures unto everlasting life, which the Son of Man will give you: for G-d the Father has set his seal upon him." Then they said to him, "What must we do in order to perform the works of G-d?" "This is the work of G-d," Jesus replied, "that you believe on the one whom he has sent." Therefore, they said to him, "What sign will you show us then, that we may see it and believe you? What will you do? Our forefathers ate manna in the desert; as it is written, 'He gave them bread from heaven to eat.'" "Most assuredly I tell you, it was not Moses who gave you the bread from heaven, but it is my Father who gives you the true bread from heaven. For the bread of G-d is he which comes down from heaven and gives life to the world." Then they said to him, "LORD, give us this bread from now on." Jesus said to them, "I am the bread of life: he who comes to me will never go hungry; and he that believes on me will never go thirsty. But, as I said to you, you have seen me and still don't believe. All that the Father gives me will come to me; and he that comes to me I will never cast out. For I did not come down from heaven to do my own will, but to do the will of him who sent me. This is the will of the Father who sent me: that I should lose none of those that he gives me, but should raise them up at the last day. It is the Father's will that everyone who sees the Son and believes on him will have everlasting life, and that I should raise them up at the last day."

Then the Jews began to murmur against him because he said, 'I am the bread that came down from heaven.' They said, "Is this not Jesus, the son of Joseph, whose father and mother we know? Then how can he say, 'I came down from heaven'?" Therefore, Jesus said to them, "Don't grumble among yourselves. No man can come to me unless the Father, who sent me, draws him; and I will raise him up at the last day. It is written in the prophets, 'They will all be taught by G-d.' Therefore, every man that has heard and learned of the Father comes to me. Not that anyone has seen the Father, except he which is of G-d, he has seen the Father. Truly, I say to you, he that believes on me has everlasting life.

"I am the Bread of Life. Your fathers ate the manna in the wilderness and are dead. This is the bread that came down from heaven, which if a man eats, he will never die. I am the living bread that came down from heaven. If anyone eats this bread he will live forever; and the bread that I give is my flesh, which I will give for the life of the world." Then the Jews began to argue among themselves, saying, "How can this man give us his flesh to eat?" Jesus said, "Truly, I tell you, that unless you eat the flesh of the Son of Man and drink his blood, you have no life in you. Whosoever eats my flesh and drinks my blood has eternal life; and I will raise him up at the last day. For my flesh is meat, and my blood is drink, indeed. He that eats my flesh and drinks my blood dwells in me, and I dwell in him. As the living Father has sent me, and I live by the Father, even so he that feeds on me will live because of me. This is the bread that came down from heaven. Unlike the manna which our forefathers ate and are dead; whoever eats this bread will live forever." He spoke of these things in the synagogue at Capernaum. Many of his disciples began to grumble, "This is a hard teaching; who can accept it?"

When Jesus became aware that his disciples were murmuring against him, he said, "Does this offend you? What if you see the Son of Man ascend up to where he was before? It is the Spirit that gives life; the flesh is counted as nothing. The words that I speak to you, they are spiritual and they are life. But, there are some of you who don't believe. Therefore, I said to you that no one can come to me unless the Father enables them." For he knew from the beginning who they were that didn't believe, and who would betray him.

From that time on, many of his disciples turned back and no longer followed him. Jesus turned to the twelve and asked, "Will you also turn away from me?" Simon Peter answered, "LORD, to whom shall we go? You have the words of eternal life. We not only believe, but we are sure that you are the Christ, the Son of the Living G-d." Then Jesus said, "Have I not chosen the twelve of you, and one of you is a devil?" He was speaking of Judas Iscariot, the son of Simon, whom he knew would betray him in time to come.

Now some of the Pharisees and teachers of the Law that had traveled from Jerusalem came to Jesus and asked, "Why is it that your disciples transgress the traditions of the elders by not washing their hands before they eat?" To this he replied, "Why do you also break the commandments of G-d by your traditions? For G-d's commandments are, 'Honor your father and mother,' and, 'he that curses his father or mother, let him be put to death.' But you say that if a man says to his father or mother, 'whatever help you might be able to receive from me is a gift wholly devoted to G-d'; and doesn't honor his father or mother with his substance, he is free from the penalty imposed by the Law. In so doing, you have made void the words of G-d for the sake of your traditions. You hypocrites! Isaiah prophesied correctly concerning you when he said:

> These people draw near to me with their mouths and honor me with their lips, but their hearts are far from me. They worship me in vain, teaching for doctrines the traditions of men.

Then Jesus called the crowd to him and said, "Listen and understand this: it is not what goes into the mouth that defiles the man. It is what comes out of the mouth that defiles the man." His disciples came to him and said, "Do you know that the Pharisees were offended when they heard these sayings?" Jesus gave this answer: "Every plant that my Heavenly Father has not planted will be uprooted. Leave them alone: they are blind leaders of the blind. If the blind leads the blind, both will fall into the ditch." Then Peter said to him, "Explain this parable to us." Jesus said, "Are you still without understanding? Don't you yet understand that whatever enters the mouth goes into the belly and is cast out of the body? But, those things that come out of the mouth, they come from the heart; and those are the things that defile a man. For out of the heart come evil thoughts, murders, adulteries, fornications, stealing, lies and blasphemies. These are the things that defile a man; but to eat with dirty hands does not defile a man."

Then Jesus left there and went into the regions of Tyre and Sidon. When he arrived, a Canaanite woman from that area came to him crying, "Have mercy upon me, O LORD, son of David; for my daughter is grievously vexed by a devil." However, Jesus never answered her with a single word. Finally, his disciples urged him to send her away because she continued to cry out after them. "I am only sent to the lost sheep of the house of Israel," he replied. Again, the woman approached Jesus and fell down at his feet. Worshiping him, she said, "LORD, please help me!" Then Jesus said to her, "It is not right to take the children's bread and throw it to the dogs." She replied, "This is true, LORD; yet the dogs eat the crumbs that fall from their masters table." At this Jesus said, "O' woman, you have strong faith. Let your desire be granted to you." In that very hour, her daughter was healed.

Jesus left that region and traveled to a place near to the Sea of Galilee, where he went up into a mountain and rested. While he was there, a great number of people came to him bringing those that were lame, blind, mute, maimed, and suffering from many other ailments; and when they left them at the foot of Jesus, he healed them all. When the people saw that all of the afflicted were healed, they glorified the G-d of Israel.

Jesus called the disciples together and said to them, "I feel compassion for these people because they have been with me for three days now, and they have nothing to eat. I don't want to send them away while they are hungry, less they collapse along the way." Then his disciples asked him, "Where can we find enough bread in this desert to feed such a large group of people?" Therefore, Jesus said to them, "How many loaves of bread do you have?" They said, "We only have seven loaves of bread and a few small fish." He instructed the people to sit on the ground. Then he took the bread and fish in his hands, gave thanks, broke them, and gave them to his disciples, who in turn distributed to the crowd. When all the people had finished eating, the disciples gathered up seven baskets full of the fragments that were left over; and the number of men that had eaten were about four thousand men, besides women and children. Dismissing the multitude, Jesus got into a ship, and sailed over to the coasts of Magdala.

Certain leaders of the Pharisee and Sadducee sects came to Jesus and tested him by asking him to show them a sign from heaven. He answered them by saying, "When evening comes you say, 'It will be fair weather,' because the sky is red. And, in the morning you say, 'It will be stormy today,' because the sky is red and overcast. You hypocrites! You can discern the appearance of the sky, yet, you cannot discern the signs of the times! A wicked and adulterous generation desires a miraculous sign; and no sign will be given to it except the sign of the prophet Jonah." Then he turned away from them and departed.

After his disciples arrived on the other side of the lake, they realized that they had forgotten to take bread. Therefore, when Jesus said to them, "Be careful, and be on your guard against the leaven of the Pharisees and Sadducees." They reasoned among themselves that he had said this because they had forgotten to take bread with them. But, when Jesus perceived this, he said to them, "O you of little faith, how can you reason within yourselves that it is because you have brought no bread that I said these words? Don't you understand yet? Don't you remember the five loaves that fed the five thousand and how many baskets of leftovers you gathered; or, the seven loaves that fed the four thousand and how many baskets of leftovers you collected? How is it that you don't understand that I was not speaking of bread when I told you that you should be on your guard against the leaven of the Pharisees and Sadducees?" Then they understood that he was not warning them to be on guard against the leaven of bread, but against the doctrines of the Pharisees and Sadducees.

When Jesus entered the coasts of Caesarea Philippi, he asked his disciples, "Who do the people say that I, the Son of Man am?" "Some of the people say you are John the Baptist," they replied. "Others say you are Elijah; and there are others who say you are Jeremiah, or one of the other prophets." "But who do you say that I am?" Jesus asked.

Then Simon Peter said to him, "You are the Christ, the Son of the living G-d!" "You are blessed, Simon bar Jonah," said Jesus, "for flesh and blood has not revealed this to you, but my Father who is in heaven. I am also telling you this: 'You are Peter.' Holding his hand to his breast, Jesus said, Upon this Rock I will build my Church; a Church that the gates of hell will not prevail against. And I will give you the keys to the Kingdom of Heaven so that whatever you bind on earth will be bound in heaven; and whatever you loose on earth will be set free in heaven." Then he commanded them not to tell anyone that he was the Christ.

From that time on Jesus began to explain to his disciples that he must go to Jerusalem and suffer many things on account of the elders, chief priests and teachers of the Law; and that he must be killed and resurrected on the third day. Then Peter took him aside and rebuked him, saying, "You are above these things LORD; these things can't happen to you!" Jesus turned to face Peter and said, "Get behind me, Satan! You are offensive to me, because you don't relish the things that are of G-d, but of men!" Then he turned to the rest of his disciples and said, "If anyone wants to come after me, he must deny himself, take up his cross and follow me. Whosoever desires to save his life will lose it; and whoever loses his life for my sake will find it. What advantage does a man have if he gains the whole world and loses his own soul? When the Son of Man comes with his angels in the glory of his Father, then he will reward every man according to his deeds. Truly I tell you, there are some standing here that will not taste of death until they see the Son of Man coming in his Kingdom."

About six days later, Jesus took Peter, James, and John his brother, and brought them up into a high mountain separate from the others. There, on the mountain, he was transfigured before them. His face shone as the sun, and his clothing became as white as the light. At that same hour, the prophets Moses and Elijah appeared before them in glorious splendor, and talked with Jesus about the work he was about to fulfill at Jerusalem. As the disciples were leaving, Peter said to Jesus, "LORD, it was good for us to be here. If you will, allow us to build three Tabernacles.; One for you, one for Moses and one for Elijah." But while he was speaking, a bright cloud enveloped them, and a voice from within the cloud said, "This is my beloved Son in whom I am well pleased; listen to him." When the disciples heard the voice, they fell on their faces before the LORD, paralyzed with fear. Jesus touched them and said, "Don't be afraid;" and when they lifted up their heads, they saw no one except Jesus.

The following day, as they were descending the mountain, Jesus instructed them not to tell the vision to anyone until after he rose from the dead. Then his disciples asked him, "Why do the teachers say that Elijah must come first?" "Elijah will come first and restore all things," Jesus replied, "but I tell you that Elijah has already come. Not only did they not recognize him; but they have done to him what they please. In like manner shall the Son of Man suffer at their hands." Then the disciples understood that he was speaking of John the Baptist.

When they came down from the mountain, they found a very large crowd waiting for them. One of the men in the crowd came to Jesus and knelt in front of him, saying,

"LORD, have mercy on my son; for he is vexed with seizures and is suffering greatly. Sometimes he falls into the fire, and sometimes into the water. I brought him to your disciples, but they could not cure him." Then Jesus said, "O faithless and perverse generation, how long shall I remain with you?! How long shall I put up with you?" Turning his attention back to the man, he said, "Bring him here to me." Then Jesus rebuked the devil and he left the boy. From that very hour the child was cured. Privately, the disciples went to Jesus and asked, "Why is it that we were unable to cast the devil out?" Jesus replied, "Because of your unbelief! I tell you the truth, if you have faith as small as a grain of mustard seed you can tell this mountain to move from here to there, and it will move. Nothing will be impossible to you. Nevertheless, this kind does not go out except through prayer and fasting."

While they were abiding in Galilee, Jesus said to them, "the Son of Man will be betrayed into the hands of men, and they will kill him; but on the third day he will be raised again." Although they didn't fully understand his words, they were filled with great sorrow.

When they arrived in Capernaum, those that collected the tribute money went to Peter and said, "Doesn't your teacher pay the Temple tax?" Peter answered them in the affirmative, but as he entered the house, Jesus detained him and asked, "Simon, what do you think? Of whom do the kings of the earth collect duty and taxes, from their own citizens or from the foreigners in their land?" "From strangers," Peter answered. "Then the citizens are exempt," Jesus said. "Notwithstanding, lest we should offend them, go to the sea and throw out your line. Look into the mouth of the first fish that comes up, and you will find a coin worth four drachmas. Take it, and give it to them for the both of us."

 At that time some of his disciples went to Jesus and asked, "Who is the greatest in the Kingdom of Heaven?" Before answering them, Jesus called a small child over to himself and had the child stand in their midst. Then he said:

> I tell you the truth, except you are converted and become as little children, you will not enter the Kingdom of Heaven. Whoever humbles himself like this little child is the greatest in the Kingdom of Heaven; and whoever receives one of these little children in my name receives me. But, whosoever entices one of these little ones that believe in me, to sin, it would be better for him if a millstone were hung around his neck and he was drowned in the depths of the sea. Woe be to the world because of the temptations of sin! Surely, temptations must come, but woe to the man through whom they come! Wherefore, if your hand or foot entices you to sin, cut them off and cast them away! It is better for you to enter life crippled or maimed, then to have two hands or two feet and be cast into everlasting fire. See that you don't despise one of these little ones; for I tell you that in heaven their angels are always looking upon the face of my Father.

The Son of Man has come to save the lost. What do you think? If a man has a hundred sheep, and one of them goes astray, does he not leave the ninety-nine and go into the mountains looking for the one that has gone astray? And, if it turns out that he finds it, I tell you the truth, he rejoices more over that one then over the ninety-nine that did not go astray. Even so, it is not the will of your heavenly Father that even one of these little ones should perish.

Moreover, if your brother does something against you, go and tell him his fault just between the two of you alone. If he will listen to you, then you have gained your brother; but if he will not listen to you, then take one or two others with you, so that every word may be firmly established in the presence of two or three witnesses. If he refuses to hear them, then tell it to the church; but if he refuses to hear the church, then treat him as you would any pagan or tax collector. Truly I tell you that whatsoever you bind on earth will be bound in heaven, and whatsoever you set free on earth will be set free in heaven. Again, I tell you that if two of you shall agree here on earth about anything they ask for, it will be done for them by my Father who is in Heaven. For where two or three are gathered in my name, there I am in the midst of them.

Then Peter stepped forward and asked him, "LORD, how often shall I forgive my brother when he sins against me, seven times? Jesus said, "No; not seven times, but seventy times seven times." Then he told them this parable:

Therefore, the Kingdom of Heaven is likened to a certain king who wanted to settle the accounts with his servants. As he began to settle, one was brought to him who owed him ten thousand talents. Since he was unable to pay, his master ordered that the man and his wife and children, as well as all his goods, be sold and the proceeds used to repay the debt. Therefore, the servant fell down at his feet and began to beg him, saying, 'LORD, please have patience with me and I will pay you all that I owe.'

Then his master was moved with compassion, forgave the debt, and set him free. But, the same servant went out and found one of his fellow servants who owed him one hundred denarii. He grabbed him and began to choke him, saying, 'Pay me what you owe me!' Unable to pay, the man fell down at his feet and pleaded with him, saying, 'Please be patient with me, and I will pay it all.' He refused and had the man thrown into prison until he could pay the debt in full.

When the other servants saw what happened they were greatly distressed, and went to tell their master all that was done to their fellow servant. Then the master called this servant in and said, 'You wicked servant! I forgave you your entire debt because you begged me; should you not have shown compassion on your fellow servant also, even as I had pity on you?' In anger, his master delivered him to the tormentors to be tortured until he paid all that he owed. My heavenly Father will do the same to you, if you, from your heart don't forgive every one of your brothers' trespasses.

Then John spoke up and said, "Master, we saw someone casting out devils in your name, and we made him stop because he was not walking with us." Jesus said to him, "Don't stop him; because he that is not against us is for us." After this, Jesus walked in Galilee rather than in Judea because he knew that the Jews were lying in wait to take his life.

As the Feast of Tabernacles drew closer, his brothers said to him, "Leave this place and go into Judea, so that your disciples can see the miracles that you are doing. For no one does his work in secret when he wants to become a public figure. If you are going to perform miracles, show yourself to the world." (His brothers didn't believe in him either). Then Jesus said, "My time has not come yet; but for you, any time is right. The world cannot hate you, but it hates me because I testify that its works are evil. You go up to the Feast; I am not going up to this Feast yet, because my time has not fully come." However, after his brothers left for the Feast, he also went, not publicly, but in secret.

The Jews were anticipating his arrival on the first day of the Feast, and wondered aloud when he did not make his appearance at the Temple. Meanwhile there was a lot of whispering among the people concerning him; for some said, "He is a good man," while others said, "No, he is a deceiver of the people." However, no one spoke of him in public because they were afraid of the Jews. About half way through the Feast, Jesus entered the Temple and began to teach. The Jews were astounded, saying, "How did this man get such knowledge, having never studied?" Jesus said to them, "My doctrine is not mine, but his that sent me. If any man chooses to do G-d's will, he will know whether the teaching comes from G-d, or whether I speak on my own accord. He that speaks his own mind does so to gain honor for himself: but he that works for the honor of the One who sent him is a man of truth, and there is no unrighteousness in him. Didn't Moses give you the Law, yet none of you keep the Law? Why are you trying to kill me?"

"You have a devil," they retorted, "who is trying to kill you?" "I have performed one miracle, and you all marvel," Jesus said. "Yet, because Moses gave you circumcision, though it didn't actually come from Moses but was handed down by the Patriarchs, you circumcise a child on the Sabbath. Now, if a child can be circumcised on the Sabbath day so that the Law of Moses is not broken; why are you angry with me because I have made a man completely whole on the Sabbath? Don't judge according to the appearance; judge with righteous judgment."

Then some of the people in Jerusalem began to ask, "Is this not the one they want to kill? But look, he is speaking boldly and they are saying nothing to him! Do the rulers know that he is the Christ? Yet, we know where this man comes from!" Then Jesus cried out in the Temple as he was teaching, "Yes, you know me, and you know where I come from. I am not here on my own, but he who sent me is true, whom you do not know. But I know him, because I came out from him, and he sent me." After he spoke these words they wanted to seize him, but no one laid a hand on him because his time had not yet come. Therefore, many of the people put their faith in him, and wondered aloud, "When the Messiah comes will he do more miracles than this man does?"

When the Pharisees heard the people saying such things about him, both they and the chief priests sent Temple officers to seize him. Jesus said to them, "I will be with you a little while longer, and then I will return to the One who sent me. You will look for me and will not be able to find me; and where I am, you cannot come." When they heard these words, the Jews began to reason among themselves, "where will he go, that we won't be able to find him? Will he go to where our people are scattered among the Gentiles, and teach the Gentiles? What did he mean when he said, 'You will look for me, and won't find me: and where I am you cannot come?'"

On the last day of the Feast, Jesus stood up and cried out, "If any man is thirsty, let him come to me and drink: for he that believes on me, as the Scripture has said, 'out of his belly shall flow rivers of living water.'" He spoke these words about the Holy Spirit whom those who believed in him would receive.

The Holy Spirit had not yet been given because Jesus had not been glorified. Therefore, when many of the people heard the statement, they said, "Surely this is the Prophet." Others said, "This is the Messiah." Still some of the others asked, "Is the Messiah supposed to come out of Galilee? Does the Scripture not say that the Messiah will come from the family of David, and from the town of Bethlehem where David lived?" So there was a division among the people because of him. Still others wanted to seize him, but no one dared lay a hand on him.

When the Temple officers returned to the chief priests and Pharisees, they asked, "Why didn't you bring him?!" The officer said, "No one's ever spoke like this man!" "Are you also deceived?!" They exclaimed. "Have any of the rulers of the Pharisees believed on him; No! Therefore, these people who don't know the Law are cursed!" Nicodemus (the Pharisee who went to see Jesus at night) said to them, "Does our Law condemn any man before it hears him and finds out what he is doing?" Then they answered him sharply, "Are you also from Galilee? Search and look! For there is no prophet that comes out of Galilee!" After this everyone left for their own house.

X.

Early the next morning when Jesus returned from the Mount of Olives, he went into the Temple. And after the people were gathered together and ready to hear him, he sat down and began to teach:

"Those who listen to the words of the Law are not the ones who are justified before G-d, but those who practice those things which are written in the Law. You who teach that a man should not commit adultery, do you commit adultery? And those of you who teach that a man should not steal, do you steal? Then why is the name of G-d blasphemed among the Gentiles because of those who boast of their obedience to the Law, if indeed you have obeyed the Law? A Jew is not one who is born a Jew in the flesh: a Jew is one who is one inwardly; one who is not only circumcised in the flesh, but is also circumcised in the heart. A circumcision that is not accomplished by one's obedience to the words of the Law, but by the work of G-d that takes place within his heart."

As he was teaching, the teachers of the Law and the Pharisees interrupted the assembly by bringing in a woman they had caught in the act of adultery. They forced her to stand in front of Jesus, and then approached him with their accusations. "Teacher," they said, "this woman was caught in the very act of adultery. Now Moses, in the Law, commanded that this type should be stoned to death; but what do you say?" They said this to tempt him, hoping that he would give them a reason to accuse him. In them was this Scripture fulfilled:

Every day they wrestle with my words: all their thoughts are against me for evil. They gather themselves together, they hide themselves, they mark my steps in wait for my soul.

Instead of answering them, Jesus bent down and began to write on the ground with his finger as though he had not heard them. When they continued to press him, he stood up and said, "The one who is without this sin among you, let him cast the first stone at her." Again, he stooped down and wrote on the ground. And they, being convicted by their own conscience, began to exit one by one, and left the woman standing there alone with Jesus.

When Jesus stood up and saw no one standing there except the woman, he said, "Woman, where are your accusers? Has no one condemned you?" She said, "No, LORD, no one." "Neither do I condemn you," Jesus answered. "Go, and sin no more."

Then Jesus turned to the people and said, "I am the Light of the world; he that follows me will never walk in darkness, but will have the light of the living." Then the Pharisees said to him, "You are testifying of yourself, therefore, your testimony isn't true." "Though I testify of myself, yet, my testimony is true," answered Jesus. "I know where I came from and I know where I am going. You judge by human standards; I don't judge anyone. Yet, if I judge, my judgment is true because I am not alone. I stand with the Father who sent me. It is written in your Law that the testimony of two men is true. I am one that bears witness of myself, and my other witness is the Father who sent me." "And, where is your Father?" They asked. "You don't know me, nor my

Father," Jesus replied, "because if you knew me you would have known my Father also."

(He was speaking to them in the Temple, near to where the offerings were placed; but no one laid their hands on him because his hour had not yet come). Jesus said to them, "I am going away, and you will look for me, and die in your sins: for where I am going, you cannot come." Then the Jews asked these questions in their hearts, "Where will he go?" "Will he kill himself?" "What does he mean, 'Where I am going, you cannot come?'" "You are from beneath: I am from above," Jesus continued. "You are of this world; I am not from this world. Therefore, I told you that you will die in your sins; because if you don't believe that I am who I say I am, you will die in your sins."

"Who are you?" They asked. Jesus said to them, "Even who I have claimed to be from the beginning. I have much to say in judgment of you: but he that sent me is true; and I will speak to the world those things which I have heard from him. When you have lifted up the Son of Man, then you will know that I am who I say that I am, and that I don't do anything on my own; but speak only what the Father has taught me."

(They didn't understand that he was referring to the Heavenly Father). "He that sent me is here with me. The Father has not left me alone; for I always do those things that please him."

As he spoke these words, many believed in him. To those who believed in him, Jesus directed these words: "If you continue in my word, then you are my disciples indeed; you will know the truth, and the truth will set you free." Then one of the Pharisees said to him, "We are the children of Abraham; we have never been in bondage to anyone! How can you say, 'You will be set free'?" "I tell you the truth." Jesus replied. "Whoever commits sin is the servant of sin. A slave is not given a permanent place in the family, only the son has a permanent place. If the Son makes you free, then you are free indeed. I know you are Abraham's children; but you want to kill me because my word has no place in you. I reveal that which I have seen with my Father; and you do that which you have seen with your father." "Abraham is our father!" They shouted. Jesus replied, "If you are Abraham's children, then you would do the things Abraham did. But now, you want to kill me, a man who has told you the truth, truth that I heard from G-d. Abraham didn't do this! You're doing the things that your own father does!"

They shouted, "We aren't the children of fornicators, the only Father we have is G-d!" "If G-d was your Father, you would love me"; Jesus retorted, "because I issued forth and came from G-d. I didn't come on my own accord, but he sent me. Why is it that you can't understand my speech? Because you cannot hear my word. Your father is the devil, and you fulfill the desires of your father. He was a murderer from the beginning, not holding to the truth, because there is no truth in him. When he tells a lie, he speaks his own language: for he is a liar and the father of it. And because I tell you the truth, you don't believe me. Which one of you convinces me to sin? And, if I am telling you the truth, why don't you believe me? He that is of G-d, believes G-d's words; therefore, you cannot hear them because you are not of G-d." Then the Jews said to him, "Are we not correct in saying that you are a Samaritan and have a devil?" Jesus replied, "I don't have a devil! I honor my Father, and you dishonor me. I am not seeking any glory for myself; there is One who seeks my glory, and he is the Judge. I tell you the truth; if a man keeps my words, he will never see death."

"Now we know you have a devil!" They shouted. Abraham and the prophets are dead; yet, you say, 'If a man keeps my words, he will never taste of death.' Are you greater than Abraham? Both he and the former prophets are dead! Who do you think you are?" To which Jesus replied, "If I honor myself, my honor means nothing; it is my Father who honors me, whom you claim is your G-d. Yet, you have not known him; but I know him. And, if I should say that I do not know him, then I would be a liar like you; but I do know him and keep his sayings. Your father Abraham rejoiced to see my day: and when he saw it, he was glad." Then the Jews said to him, "You are not even fifty years old, and you have seen Abraham?" Then Jesus said, "Before Abraham was born, I am." At this, they picked up stones to throw at him, but Jesus hid himself and slipped away from the Temple.

As Jesus walked along with his disciples, he said to them: "Come near to me and listen to what I say; I have not spoken in secret from the beginning: from before time was, there am I; and the Father, by his Spirit, has sent me. I am the First, and I am also the Last. I have been sent to a people that have been rebellious from the beginning, even as it was written concerning me,"

Son of man, I am sending you to the children of Israel, to a rebellious nation that has rebelled against me.

"Search the Scriptures: the penalty for rebellion and unbelief, which is sin, is death. Therefore, I lay down my life, that whosoever comes to me will not die, but have eternal life."

As they continued on their journey, they came upon a man who had been blind since birth. His disciples asked him, "Rabbi, who sinned, this man or his parents, that he was born blind?" "Neither this man, nor his parents sinned" Jesus replied. "This happened so that the work of G-d would be manifested in his life. I must fulfill the works of the One who sent me while the day remains. The night is coming when no one can work. As long as I am in the world, I am the Light of the world." After he said this, he spat on the ground, made some mud with the spittle, and put it on the eyes of the blind man. Then he said to the man, "Go, wash your eyes in the pool of Siloam. So the man went and washed the clay from his eyes, and returned home with his eyesight. His neighbors and those who had known him to be blind all his life said, "Is he not the one who used to sit and beg?" Some said that it was the same man; others said that he looked like him: but he said, "I am the one." "How did you receive your sight?" They asked. He answered, "a man named Jesus made some clay and anointed my eyes; then he told me to go and wash my eyes in the pool of Siloam. So I went and washed, and I received my sight." Then they asked him, "Where is he?" But, he told them that he didn't know. Then they brought him to the Pharisees because it was upon the Sabbath day that Jesus had made the mud and caused the man to receive his sight. The Pharisees also asked him how he received his sight. "He put mud on my eyes, and I washed it off, and now I see!" The man replied. Some of the Pharisees said, this man is not of G-d because he doesn't observe the Sabbath day." Others said, "How can a sinner perform such miracles?" Consequently, there was a division among them. Turning back to the man who was previously blind, they said, "What do you say about him since he has opened your eyes?" The man said, "He is a prophet." However, the Jews didn't believe the report that he had been born blind and then suddenly received his sight, until after they had summoned his parents. "Is this your son?" They asked. "Is this the same one whom you say was born blind? How come he can see now?" His parents answered and said, "We know that this is our son, and that he was born blind; but by what means he can see now, we don't know; neither do we know who opened his eyes. He is of age; ask him: he can speak for himself." His parents spoke like this because they feared the Jews. The Jews had already decided that if anyone confessed that Jesus was the Messiah they would be put out of the synagogue permanently. Once again, they summoned the man who had been blind and said to him, "Give G-d the praise; we know this man is a sinner!" The man spoke up and said, "Whether he is a sinner or not, I don't know. The only thing I know is this; I used to be blind, but now I can see." Again they questioned him, what did he do to you; and how did he open your eyes?" He responded by saying, "I have told you already, and you didn't listen; so why do you want to hear it again: are you going to be his disciples?" Then they began to mock him saying, "You are his disciple! We are Moses' disciples! We know that G-d spoke to Moses; but as for this fellow, we don't know where he comes from!" Then the man said to them, "Isn't this remarkable? You don't know where he comes from, yet he opened my eyes. Now we know that G-d doesn't listen to sinners! He will only listen to those who worship him and fulfill his will. Since the world began, no one has ever heard of a man who could open the eyes of the blind. If this man was not of G-d, he could do nothing!" Then they said to him, "You were born in sins, and you are going to teach us!?" Then they excommunicated him from the Temple. When Jesus heard that they had excommunicated him, he looked for him. And when he found him, he said to the man, "Do you believe on the Son of G-d?" "Who is he, LORD, that I might believe on him?" The man asked. "You have seen him," Jesus said, "and it is the one who is talking to you." The man replied, "LORD, I believe." Then he prostrated himself at the feet of Jesus and worshiped him. Jesus said, "For judgment have I come into this world so that the blind may see; and so that those who see might be made blind." There were some Pharisees with him which heard these words, and they said, "Are we blind also?" "If you were blind, you would have no sin," Jesus said. "But since you say that you can see, your sin remains upon you." Then he continued with this teaching:

> Before one can proclaim the truth of Scripture, he must first be able to 'see' it. In describing the prophets of old, it is written, 'Before time, they were called Seers.' If a man testifies before the Council and declares what he believes to be the truth of the matter, though he has never seen nor heard anything himself, is his testimony not dismissed as mere hearsay or opinion, and he rejected as a true witness?

> No man can see, nor hear, the words of G-d unless G-d first causes his light to shine upon them and opens their eyes. In this way, he reveals himself to them, and they become true witnesses; declaring only those things which they have both seen and heard. By the light of G-d, the prophets 'saw' the

truth; examined and approved the things they 'saw' that they were true, and then professed to others. 'This is what the LORD has said, 'and, as long as they continued to abide in his light they were able to see and to hear those things that pertained to the Kingdom of G-d.

I don't testify of what I believe to be true; neither do I give an unfounded opinion of the truth. I only testify of what I have both seen and heard from my Father; therefore, my testimony is valid, and I am a true witness. Wherefore, I said to you, 'If you knew me, you would have already known my Father.' Why do I say that? Because you would be walking in his light. No one knows who the Son is, but the Father; and it is my Father's pleasure to reveal him. If you did know the Father, then you would know me, because he testifies of me; and you would know that my testimony is true. Why can't you accept my testimony? Because you don't know him: neither do you walk in his light. You are blind and walk in the darkness of your father. Likewise, I will tell you this he that does not enter through the gate into the sheep fold, but climbs up some other way, is a thief and a robber. But he that enters through the door is the Shepherd of the sheep, for whom the Porter opens the gate. The sheep, whom he knows by name, listen for his voice, and as he leads them out he walks ahead of them; and the sheep follow him because they know his voice. They won't follow a stranger, but will run from him, because they won't acknowledge the voice of strangers.

(They didn't understand what he was trying to say).

I tell you the truth, I am the door of the sheep. All that ever came before me were thieves and robbers; but the sheep didn't recognize them. I am the door: if any man enters through me, he will be saved, and will go in and out freely and find pasture. The thief doesn't come unless he wants to steal, kill, or destroy; but I have come that they might have life, and have it much more abundantly.

I am the good shepherd. The good shepherd lays down his life for the sheep. The hired hand is not the shepherd who owns the sheep; therefore, when he sees the wolf coming, he abandons the sheep and runs away. Then the wolf attacks the sheep and scatters them. The hired hand flees because he is a hired hand and cares nothing for the sheep. I am the good shepherd; I know my sheep and they know me even as the Father knows me and I know the Father, and I lay down my life for the sheep. I have other sheep which are not of this fold whom I must also bring. They too will listen to my voice. Then, there will be one flock and one shepherd. Therefore, my Father loves me because I surrender my life for the sheep; only to raise it up again. No one takes it from me, I lay it down of my own accord. I have the power to lay it down, and I have the power to raise it up again. I have received this authority from my Father.

Once again, there was a division among the Jews. Many of them said, "He is demon possessed and raving mad! Why do you listen to him?" Others said, "These are not the words of a man who is demon possessed! Besides, can the devil open the eyes of the blind?"

Then came the Feast of the Dedication at Jerusalem, and it was winter. As Jesus walked in the Temple, in Solomon's colonnade, the Jews surrounded him and said, "How long are you going to keep us in suspense? If you are the Messiah, tell us plainly!" "I have told you already, and you didn't believe me," Jesus replied. "The miracles I do in my Father's name, they speak for me; otherwise, would I not come under the same condemnation as you? Remember the word of the LORD to the prophet Ezekiel:

> *Son of man, prophesy against the shepherds of Israel: prophesy and say unto them, thus said the LORD G-d to the shepherds; woe be to the shepherds of Israel who feed themselves! Should the shepherds not feed the flock? You eat the fat, clothe yourselves with their wool, and kill them that are fed, but you do not feed the flock. You have not strengthened the diseased, neither have you healed the sick, or, bound up that which is broken. You have not brought back those who have been driven away, neither did you look for them; instead, you have ruled over them with force and cruelty; and they were scattered because there is no shepherd.*

"But, as I have already said to you, you don't believe because you are not of my sheep. My sheep know my voice; I know them, and they follow me. To them I give eternal life, and they will never perish; neither can anyone snatch them out of my hand. My Father, who gave them to me, is greater than all; and no one is able to snatch them out of his hand. I and the Father are one."

(Then the Jews picked up stones to stone him).

"Many great miracles have I shown you from my Father; for which one of these miracles are you stoning me?" Jesus asked. "We are not stoning you for any miracle! We are stoning you for blasphemy! Because you, being a man, make yourself G-d!" They explained. Then Jesus responded by saying, "Is it not written in your Law, 'I have said, you are G-ds'? If he called them 'G-ds,' to whom the word came – and the Scriptures can't be broken – how can you say to him, whom the Father has sanctified and sent into the world, that he is blaspheming? Just because I said that I am the Son of G-d? If I am not doing the miracles of my Father, don't believe me! But if I do, even if you don't believe me, believe the miracles! This way you will know, and believe, that the Father is in me, and I am in the Father!" Again they tried to seize him, but he escaped their grasp. Then Jesus traveled across the Jordan to the place where John first baptized, and resided there. Many of the people continued to turn to him, and many more believed in him, saying, "John didn't perform any miracles, but everything he said about this man is certainly true."

XI.

Jesus had a close friend named Lazarus, who lived in Bethany with his two sisters, Mary and Martha. (This was the same Mary who anointed the LORD with ointment, and wiped his feet with her hair). When Lazarus became very ill, his sisters sent this message to Jesus, "LORD, the one you love is sick." When Jesus received the message, he said, "This sickness is not for death, but for the glory of G-d, so that the Son of G-d might be glorified by it." Now Jesus loved Lazarus and his sisters dearly. But after he received the message, he decided to extend his departure time and to remain in the same place a little longer.

At the end of three days he said to his disciples, "Let us go into Judea again." Startled by his words, they replied, "Master, not too many days ago, the Jews tried to stone you, and you want to go back there again?!" Jesus replied, "Are there not twelve hours in the day? If a man walks in the daylight he will not stumble, because he can see where he is going. But, when he walks at night he stumbles because there is no light." After he said these things, he went on to say, "Our friend Lazarus is sleeping; but I am going to wake him from his sleep." Then his disciples said to him, "LORD, if he sleeps, he will get well." They thought he was speaking of restful sleep, but Jesus was referring to his death. "Lazarus is dead," Jesus said. "And, I am glad that I didn't go there for your sakes, so that you might believe. Nevertheless, let us go to him." Then Thomas (called Didymus) said to the rest of the disciples, "Let us go with him so that we can die with him also."

Upon his arrival in Bethany, which is only about two miles away from Jerusalem, Jesus found that Lazarus had already been in the tomb for four days, and that many of the Jews had visited Mary and Martha to comfort them over the loss of their brother. When Martha heard that Jesus was coming, she ran out to meet him, leaving Mary at home. She said to Jesus, "LORD, if you would have been here, my brother would not have died. But I know that even now, whatever you ask of G-d, he will give it to you." Jesus said to her, "Your brother will surely rise again." Martha said to him, "I know he will rise again in the resurrection on the last day." "I am the resurrection and the life," Jesus said. "He that believes in me will never die. Do you believe this?" "Yes, LORD," Martha replied. "And I also believe that you are the Christ, the Son of G-d, who was supposed to come into the world."

After she spoke these words, she ran back and called Mary aside and said, "The Master has arrived, and he is calling for you." Mary rose up immediately and went to meet him at the same place where Martha had met him, for Jesus had not yet entered the village.

When the Jews saw Mary rise up quickly and run out, they followed after her, thinking she was going to the grave site to mourn there. But when Mary reached the place where Jesus was, she fell at his feet and said, "LORD, if you would have been here, my brother would not have died." When Jesus saw her crying, and the Jews who had come along with her also crying, he groaned in the spirit and was deeply moved. "Where have you buried him?" He asked. "LORD, come and see" they answered. Jesus began to weep. When the Jews saw him crying, they said, "See how much he loved him!" But some of them said, "Couldn't this man, who opens the eyes of the blind, have prevented him from dying?" Once again, Jesus groaned in his spirit as he approached the grave. It was a cave, with a stone laid across its entrance. Speaking to the men standing by, Jesus said, "Take the stone away."

Astonished at his command to remove the stone, Mary said, "LORD, by this time the odor is bad because he's been there for four days!" "Didn't I tell you that if you would believe, you would see the glory of G-d?" Jesus asked. When they took the stone away from the cave, Jesus looked up toward heaven and said, "Father, I thank you for hearing me; and I know that you always hear me, but because of the people that are standing here I said it, so that they may believe that you have sent me." After he said these words, he cried out in a loud voice, "Lazarus, come out!" Moments later, Lazarus emerged from the grave bound hand and foot with strips of linen, and a cloth wrapped about his face. Then Jesus said to them, "Loose him, and let him go." Therefore, many of the Jews which had gone with Mary to the tomb, and had witnessed the things that he did, believed on him.

Nevertheless, some of them went to the Pharisees and told them what Jesus had done. After hearing the account of Lazarus, they called an emergency meeting of the Sanhedrin. "What are we going to do?" They queried. "This man is performing all these miracles, and if we leave him alone, everyone will believe on him; then the Romans will come and take away our Temple and our nation!" One of them named Caiaphas, who was the high priest that year, spoke up, "Don't you know anything at all? Don't you realize that it is better to let one man die for the people, then to let the whole nation perish?" He didn't say this on his own, but as the high priest that year he prophesied that Jesus should die for the nation; and not for the Jewish nation alone, but also that he would gather together the children of G-d that were scattered abroad and make them one. So, from that day forward they plotted his death. For which cause, Jesus no longer walked about publicly among the Jews, but he withdrew from there and travelled to a village near the desert called Ephraim, where he stayed with his disciples.

As the time approached for him to be taken up to heaven, he was resolved to return to Jerusalem. Wherefore, he sent messengers ahead of him to a village of the Samaritans to get things ready. But, they refused to welcome him because he appeared to be headed towards Jerusalem. When James and John, his disciples, saw this they asked, "LORD, do you want us to call fire down from heaven and consume them, like Elijah did?" Turning about abruptly, he rebuked them saying, "You don't know what kind of spirit you are of! The Son of man didn't come to destroy men's lives, but to save them!"

As they were walking towards another village, they met a man who said to him, "LORD, I will follow you wherever you go." Jesus answered, "The foxes have holes to live in and the birds have nests, but the Son of Man has no place to lay his head." Then he said to another, "Follow me." But he said, "LORD, permit me to go and bury my father first." "Let the dead bury their dead;" Jesus replied. "But you go and preach the kingdom of G-d." Another man said to him, "I will follow you; but let me first go and say goodbye to my family." To him Jesus said, "no man who puts his hand to the plow and looks back, is suitable for the Kingdom of G-d." After this the LORD appointed seventy others and sent them ahead of him, two by two, into every town and place where he was intending to go. Then he said to them,

> Truly, the harvest is plentiful, but the laborers are few. Pray, and ask the LORD of the Harvest to send forth laborers into his harvest. Go your way. I am sending you out like lambs among wolves. Don't take a purse, or scrip, nor sandals; and don't salute anyone on the road. Whatever house you enter, first say, 'Peace be to this house.' If the man of peace is there, your peace will rest upon him; if not, it will return to you. Remain in the same house, eating and drinking whatever they put in front of you; for the worker is worthy of his wages. Don't go from house to house. Into whatever city you enter, and are welcomed, eat whatever is put in front of you. Heal the sick that are therein, and say to them, 'the Kingdom of G-d is near.' But whenever you enter a town and they don't welcome you, go out into the streets and say, 'Even the very dust of your town that sticks to our feet do we shake off as a sign against you! But understand this: The Kingdom of G-d is near!' I tell you, it will be more tolerable in that day for Sodom, then for that city.

> Woe to you, Chorazin! Woe to you, Bethsaida! For if the mighty works which had been done in you had been done in Tyre and Sidon, they would have repented long ago in sackcloth and ashes! But, it will be more tolerable for Tyre and Sidon at the judgment than for you! And you, Capernaum, which is exalted

to the heavens, you will be cast down to hell! He that listens to you, listens to me; and he that despises you, despises me; and he that despises me, despises him that sent me.

When the seventy returned, they were ecstatic and exclaimed, "LORD, even the devils submit to us through your name!" Jesus said to them, "I saw Satan fall from heaven like a bolt of lightning. I have given you the authority to trample on snakes and scorpions, and over all the powers of the enemy; and by no means will anything hurt you. However, don't rejoice in the fact that the spirits are submitting to you; but rejoice in this, that your names are written in heaven."

In that same hour Jesus rejoiced in the Spirit, and said, "I thank you, Father, LORD of heaven and earth, that you have hidden these things from the wise and prudent and have revealed them to children! Yes, Father, even because it was your good pleasure!"

"All things have been committed to me by my Father," Jesus said. "No one knows who the Son is except the Father; or, who the Father is except the Son, and those to whom the Son will reveal him to." Then in a lower voice he said to his disciples, "Blessed are the eyes that see the things which you see; for I tell you, many prophets and kings have desired to see the things which you see, and have not seen them, and to hear the things which you have heard and have not heard them."

On another occasion, a certain lawyer confronted Jesus to test him: "Teacher," he asked, "what must I do to inherit eternal life?" "What is written in the Law?" Jesus asked.

"How do you read it?" The lawyer answered, "You shall love the LORD, your G-d, with all your heart, with all your soul, with all your strength and with all your mind; and your neighbor as yourself." Jesus replied, "You have answered correctly; do this and you will live." But, willing to justify the question, the lawyer asked, "Who is my neighbor?" In response Jesus said, "A man was traveling from Jerusalem to Jericho when he fell into the hands of thieves who stripped him of his clothing, beat him and went away, leaving him half dead. By chance a certain priest traveled down the same road; and when he saw the man, he crossed over to the other side of the road and kept walking. Likewise, a Levite happened to pass that way, and when he saw the man, he also crossed over to the other side of the road and kept walking. But when a certain Samaritan, who was traveling on the same road, saw him, he had compassion on the man and went over to him. He bandaged up his wounds, pouring oil and wine on them. Then he put the man on his donkey, took him to an inn and took care of him. The next morning, he gave the innkeeper two denarii, and said, 'Take care of him; and if it costs you more than this, I will repay you when I return.' Which one of these three do you think was his neighbor?" He said, "The one who showed mercy." Then Jesus told him, "You go and do the same."

Jesus and his disciples entered the village where Martha received him into her house. Her sister, Mary, sat at the feet of Jesus and listened to his every word while she was busy preparing and serving the food. Finally, Martha went to Jesus and said, "LORD, don't you care that my sister has left me by myself to serve alone? Tell her please, that she should be helping me." "Martha, Martha," the LORD answered, "you are worried and upset about so many things; but there is only one thing that is really important, and Mary has chosen it; therefore, I will not take it away from her."

One day, after Jesus finished praying, one of his disciples said to him, "LORD, teach us how to pray, just as John taught his disciples." Therefore, Jesus said to them, "When you pray, say:

> *Our Father in heaven, hallowed be your name. Let your kingdom come, and let your will be done here on earth, even as it is in heaven. Give us, day by day, our daily bread, and forgive us our sins, for we also forgive everyone that sins against us. Lead us away from temptation, and deliver us from evil. Amen."*

"Which one of you would have a friend, to whom you would go at midnight and say, 'Friend, loan me three loaves of bread; because a friend of mine has traveled to see me and I don't have anything to set before him.' And he, from inside, answers, 'Don't bother me; the door is already locked, and the children are with me in bed, so I can't get up and give you anything.' No; I tell you, though he may not want to get up and give to you out of friendship, yet because of your persistence he will get up and give you as much as you need. Therefore, I say to you: Ask, and it will be given to you; Seek, and you will find; Knock, and the door will be opened to you. Which of you fathers, if your son asks you for bread, will give him a stone? Or, if he asks you for a fish, will give him a serpent instead? Or, if he asks for an egg, will hand him a scorpion? If you then, being evil, know how to give good gifts to your children, how much more will your Heavenly Father give the Holy Spirit to those who ask him?"

It came to pass that Jesus cast the devil out of a man that was mute, and when the demon left him he was able to speak; a feat that left the crowd completely astonished. But, some of the Jews that were present said, "He casts out devils through Beelzebub, the Prince of the devils." Still others, trying to tempt him, desired a miraculous sign from heaven. But Jesus said to them:

> Every kingdom divided against itself will collapse, and a house divided against itself will fall. If Satan is also divided against himself, how can his kingdom stand? I am asking you this because you say that I am casting out devils by Beelzebub. And, if I am casting out devils by Beelzebub, then by whom are your sons casting them out? Therefore, let them be your judges. But, if I cast out devils by the finger of G-d, no doubt the Kingdom of G-d has come to you. When a strong man arms himself and secures his palace, then his goods are safe. But, when someone stronger than him attacks and overpowers him, he takes away the armor that he trusted in and divides up his goods. He that is not with me is against me: and he that doesn't gather with me scatters abroad. When the unclean spirit leaves a man, it walks through dry places, seeking rest, but is unable to find it. Then it says, 'I will return to the house that I left;' and when it returns, it finds it swept, clean and in order. Then he goes and takes seven other spirits more wicked than itself, and they enter in and dwell there; and the last state of that man is worse than the first.

A woman in the crowd cried out, "Blessed is the womb that bore you and the breast that nursed you!" Jesus replied,

"Yes, but blessed are they that hear the Word of G-d and practice it."

(As he saw the crowds increasing in number, Jesus said):

This is an evil generation. It asks for a miracle; but none will be given to it except the sign of Jonah. For as Jonah was a sign to the Ninevites, so shall the Son of Man be to this generation also. The Queen of the South will rise up in the judgment against the people of this generation and condemn them, because she came from a far distance to hear the wisdom of Solomon; and one greater than Solomon is here. And the Ninevites will rise up in judgment against this generation and condemn it, because they repented at the teaching of Jonah; and look, one greater than Jonah is here.

No one lights a candle and puts it in a hiding place, or under a basket. Instead, he puts it on a candlestick, so that those who come in may see the light. The light of the body is the eye. Therefore, when your eye is clear your whole body is full of light. But when your eye is bad, your body is full of darkness. Make sure that the light in you isn't wickedness. If your whole body is full of light, no part of which is dark, it will be completely lit as when the light of a candle shines upon you.

As he was speaking, a certain Pharisee invited Jesus to dine with him. Jesus accepted his invite, followed him into the house and reclined at the table. When the Pharisee realized that he had sat down to eat without first washing his hands, he marveled. The LORD said to him, "You Pharisees are so careful about making sure the outside of the cup and the platter is clean; yet, don't consider that the inward part is full of greed and malice. You fool! Didn't the one who made the outside of the dish, make the inside part as well? Give that which is inside the dish to the poor, and everything else will be considered clean for you. Woe to you Pharisees! For you tithe mint, rue and all types of garden herbs to G-d, but neglect to teach the love of G-d and his judgments! You should have practiced the latter without leaving the former undone. Woe to you Pharisees! How you love to sit in the most important seats in the synagogues and to have the greetings of the people in the marketplace! Woe to you scribes and Pharisees, hypocrites! You are like unmarked graves which men walk over without knowing it!"

Then one of the lawyers spoke up and said, "Teacher, when you say such things, you are insulting us also.

Woe to you lawyers also!" Jesus countered. "You load people down with burdens too heavy to bear, but you yourselves will not lift a finger to help them! Woe be to you! Because you build tombs for the prophets, and it was your forefathers who killed them! By your actions, you are testifying that you approve of the deeds of your forefathers: for they killed them, and you build their tombs! Therefore, in his wisdom, G-d said, 'I will send them my prophets and apostles, though some they will kill and others they will persecute.' So then, this generation will be held responsible for the blood of all the prophets that has been shed since the foundation of the world; from the blood of righteous Abel to the blood of Zechariah, who was killed between the altar and the sanctuary. Yes, I tell you, the people of this generation will be held responsible for the shedding of their blood!

Woe to you lawyers! For you have taken away the key of knowledge! You yourselves have not entered in, and you have hindered those who were trying to enter.

Then Jesus arose from his seat to leave that place. But as he was leaving, the Pharisees and teachers of the Law began to oppose him fiercely, trying to provoke him to answer questions and to comment inadvisably, so that they might be able to accuse him.

Meanwhile, many thousands of people had gathered together, so much so, that they were trampling upon one another. Then Jesus spoke to his disciples first, saying:

Beware of the yeast of the Pharisees, which is hypocrisy: there is nothing concealed that will not be disclosed, and there is nothing hidden, that will not be made known. Whatever you have spoken in the dark will be heard in the light; and what you have whispered in the ear in a secret place will be proclaimed from the rooftops. Furthermore, I tell you this my friends: do not be afraid of those who can kill the body, and are powerless to do anything more. But I will show you whom you should fear: fear him who, after killing the body, has the power to cast you into hell. Yes, I tell you, fear him.

Are five sparrows not sold for two pennies? Yet, not one of them is forgotten by G-d. Indeed, the very hairs of your head are all numbered. Therefore, don't be afraid; You are worth more than many sparrows. I will also tell you this: whosoever will confess me before men, I will confess him before the Angels of G-d. But he that will disown me before men, him will I disown before the Angels of G-d. If anyone speaks a word against the Son of Man, he will be forgiven; but if anyone blasphemes against the Holy Ghost, he will never be forgiven.

So, when they bring you before the synagogues, rulers and authorities, do not worry about how you are going to defend yourselves, or what you are going to say; because the Holy Spirit will teach you at that time what you are going to say.

Then someone in the crowd said to him, "Teacher, speak to my brother, and tell him to divide the inheritance with me." Jesus retorted, "Man, who made me a judge or an arbitrator over you?" Then Jesus turned to his disciples and told them this parable:

Watch out, and beware of greed; because a man's life does not consist in the abundance of the things he has in his possession. Listen to the story of a certain rich man: The ground of this rich man produced a plentiful crop. So he said to himself, 'What should I do? I don't have enough room to store my crops.' Then he said, 'I know what I will do: I will tear down my barns and build bigger ones to store my grain and my goods.' Then I will say to myself, 'you have plenty of good things laid up for many years; take life easy; eat, drink and be merry.' But, G-d said to him, 'You fool, tonight your life will be required of you. Then who will get what you have preserved for yourself?' This is how it is with anyone who stores up treasures for himself and is not rich toward G-d. Therefore, I tell you, don't worry about your life, as to what you will eat; neither for the body, what you will put on. Life is more important than food, and the body is more valuable than clothing. Consider the ravens: they neither plant, nor do they harvest; and they don't have storehouses or barns; yet G-d feeds them. How much more valuable are you to G-d than the birds? Which one of you by worrying, can add one single cubit to his height? If you are unable to do this small thing, why worry about the rest?

Consider the lilies and how they grow. They don't labor, nor do they spin. Yet, I tell you that Solomon, in all his splendor, was not dressed like one of these. So then, if G-d clothes the grass, which is in the field today and burnt in the fire tomorrow, how much more will he clothe you? O' you of little faith! Don't set your mind on what you will eat or drink, neither be doubtful, for all the people of the world run after such things, and your Father already knows that you need them. Rather, seek the Kingdom of G-d, and all these things will be given to you.

Don't be afraid, little flock, for it is your Father's desire to give you the kingdom. Sell your possessions and give to the poor. Store up for yourselves bags that can't wear out, treasures in heaven that cannot be depleted; where no thief can get near, nor any moth destroy. For where your treasure is, that is where your heart will be also.

Be fully dressed and have your lamps burning, like men who are waiting for their master to return from a wedding; so that when he returns and knocks, you can immediately open the door for him. Those servants, whom the master finds watching when he returns, will be blessed. In truth I tell you, he will dress himself to serve, have them recline at the table, and serve them himself. This he will do for his servants, even if he comes in the second or third watch of the night.

Understand this, if the head of the house knew what hour the thief was coming, he would watch and would not allow his house to be broken into. Therefore, you be ready also, for the Son of Man will come at a time when you're not expecting him.

Then Peter said to him, "LORD, are you speaking this parable to us, or to everyone?" The LORD answered with another parable:

Who is the faithful and wise steward, whom the master shall appoint to take charge over his household to give them their portion of food at the proper time? It is that servant who will be blessed when his master returns and finds him fulfilling his duties. I tell you, truthfully, he will put that servant in charge of all his possessions.

But, if the servant says in his heart, 'My master's return has been delayed,' and he begins to mistreat the menservants and women servants, and to eat and drink and get drunk. That servant's master will return on a day when he is not expecting him, and at an hour that he is not aware of. Then he will cut him to pieces and assign him a place with the unbelievers.

That servant who knows his master's will and doesn't prepare himself, nor fulfills the will of his master, will be beaten with many stripes. But, the one who does not know, yet does things worthy of punishment will be beaten with a few stripes. From everyone to whom much has been given, much will be required; and from him to whom men have entrusted much, more will be asked of him.

I have come to send fire on the earth: and what purpose will I serve if it is already kindled? But, I have a baptism to undergo, and how distressed I am until it is accomplished! Do you think that I have come to bring peace on the earth? I tell you, no. Instead, I have come to bring division. From now on, there will be five in one house divided, three against two, and two against three. The father will stand against his own son, and the son will stand against his father. The mother will stand against her daughter, and the daughter will stand against her mother. The mother-in-law and daughter-in-law will also stand against each other.

(Then, he directed these words to the Pharisees),

When you see a cloud rising out of the west, right away you say that it's going to rain, and it does. When the wind blows from the south, you say that it will be hot, and so it is. You hypocrites! You can interpret the appearance of the sky and of the earth and make sound predictions! Yet, you can't interpret the present time!

Why don't you judge for yourself what is right? When you are going with your adversary before the magistrate, you should try very hard to be reconciled with him on the way; otherwise, he will drag you off to the judge, who in turn will deliver you to the officer to be thrown into prison. I tell you, you won't be released from there until you have paid the last penny.

There were some there who told Jesus about the Galileans, whose blood Pilate had mixed with their sacrifices. Jesus answered thus:

Do you think that these Galileans were worse sinners than all the other Galileans because they suffered such things? I tell you, no! But, unless you repent, you will all perish. Or, those eighteen who were killed when the tower of Siloam fell upon them; do you think they were greater sinners than all the other men who resided in Jerusalem? I tell you, no! But, unless you repent, you will all perish.

A certain man had a fig tree planted in his vineyard, and when he went looking for fruit on it, he didn't find any. Then he said to the caretaker of his vineyard, 'Listen, for three years now I have come looking for fruit on this tree and haven't found any. Cut it down! Why should it use up the soil?' The caretaker said, 'LORD, leave it alone for one more year, and I'll dig around it and fertilize it. If it yields fruit, fine. If not, then cut it down.'

As Jesus was teaching in the synagogue on the Sabbath, he noticed a woman who was bent over and couldn't raise herself up; for she had been crippled by a spirit of infirmity for eighteen years. He called her over to himself and said,

"Woman, you are loosed from your infirmity." Then he laid his hands on her, and immediately she was able to stand upright, and began to glorify G-d. However, since Jesus had healed her on the Sabbath, the ruler of the synagogue responded with indignation and said to the people, "There are six days when men should work; come on those days and be healed, not on the Sabbath." "You hypocrite!" Jesus scowled. "Don't each one of you, on the Sabbath day, loose his ox or donkey from the stall and lead it out to give it water? Shouldn't this woman, being a daughter of Abraham, whom Satan has bound these eighteen years, be loosed from this bond on the Sabbath?" After he said these things, all of his adversaries were ashamed, and the people rejoiced because of all the mighty things which were done by him.

Then he said, "What is the Kingdom of G-d like? What can I compare it to? It is like a grain of mustard seed which a man took and planted in his garden; and it grew and became a large tree, so that the birds came and perched in its branches.

"What is the Kingdom of G-d like? It is like yeast, which a woman took and mixed into three measures of meal, until it worked all through the dough." Turning away from the crowd, Jesus continued on his journey to Jerusalem. As he journeyed, he stopped to teach in every town and village he passed through on the way.

XII.

Someone asked Jesus, "LORD, will only a few be saved?" And he answered him, saying, "Make every attempt to enter in at the narrow gate: for I tell you that many will try to enter in and will not be able to. Once the master of the house gets up and shuts the door, there will be many standing outside knocking and pleading with him, 'LORD! LORD! Open the door!' And from inside, he will answer, 'I don't know who you are, nor where you come from.' Then they will begin to say, 'LORD, we ate and drank in your presence, and you taught in our streets!' But he will reply, 'I told you, I don't know who you are, nor where you come from; depart from me, all you evildoers!'

"There will be weeping and gnashing of teeth when you see Abraham, Isaac, and Jacob, and all the prophets in the Kingdom of G-d, but you yourselves thrown out. People will come from the east and west, north and south, and sit down in the Kingdom of G-d. And there will be those who are last who will be first, and first who will be last."

That same day, certain Pharisees went out to see him and said,' "Get out of here and leave this place! Herod wants to kill you!" "You go and tell that fox" Jesus replied, "I will cast out devils and heal people today and tomorrow, and on the third day I will accomplish my task. I must continue to walk today, tomorrow and the next day; for it cannot be that a prophet dies outside of Jerusalem. O' Jerusalem! Jerusalem! You who kill the prophets and stone those who are sent to you; how often I have wanted to gather your children together, as a hen gathers her chicks under her wings, but you weren't willing! Look! Your house is left desolate! I tell you, you will not see me again until you say, 'Blessed is he that comes in the name of the LORD.'"

On one particular Sabbath Jesus went to eat at the house of a prominent Pharisee. They watched him carefully, for there in front of him was a man suffering from dropsy. Knowing that their eyes were fastened upon him, Jesus asked the Pharisees and lawyers, "Is it lawful to heal on the Sabbath?" When they held their peace, he laid hands on the man, healed him and sent him away. Then, turning his attention back to them he said, "Which one of you, having an ox or donkey fall into a pit, will not immediately pull it out on the Sabbath?" Not one of them dared answer him a word. When he noticed that the guests picked the chief places of honor at the table, he spoke this parable:

When someone invites you to a wedding, don't sit down in the place of honor, because someone more distinguished than you may have been invited. If you do, and the host who invited both of you comes over to you and says, 'Give this man your seat;' you will be humiliated in front of the other guests as you arise and take the lesser seat. But when you are invited, go and sit in the lesser seat, so that when the host comes and says to you, 'Friend move up to the better seat.' You will have honor in the presence of all the other invited guests. For whosoever exalts himself will be humbled, and he that humbles himself will be exalted.

(Then he said to the Pharisee that had invited him),

When you prepare a dinner or supper, don't call your friends, brothers, or relatives, nor your rich neighbors. If you do, they may invite you back, and thus you have been repaid. Instead, invite the poor, the maimed, the lame and the blind. Then you will be blessed, because they cannot repay you. You will surely be repaid at the resurrection of the just.

When one of those at the table heard these words, he said to Jesus, "Blessed is he that shall eat bread in the Kingdom of G-d." To this Jesus replied:

A certain man was preparing a great supper and invited many guests. When the feast was ready, he sent one of his servants to tell those who had been invited, 'Come; for everything is ready.' But they all began to make excuses. The first said, 'I have just purchased a piece of ground, and I must go and see it; Please excuse me.' Another said, 'I have bought five yoke of oxen, and I am going to try them out; please have me excused.' Another said, 'I just got married, so I cannot come.' Therefore, when the servant went back and reported these things to his master, his master became angry and said to his servant, 'Go out quickly into the streets and lanes of the city and bring in the poor, the crippled, the lame and the blind.' When the servant returned to his master, he said, 'Master, everything was done as you commanded it, but there is still room.' Then the master gave him this command, 'Go out into the roadways and country lanes and compel them to come in, so that my house may be full. For I tell you that none of those men who were invited will taste of my supper.'

When he left the Pharisee's house, a large crowd followed after him; to whom he turned and said:

If anyone comes to me, and does not love his father and mother, wife and children, brothers and sisters, less than me; yes, even his own life as well, he cannot be my disciple. And anyone who does not bear his cross and come after me, cannot be my disciple.

Which one of you, intending to build a tower, will not first sit down and estimate the cost, to see if he has enough to finish it? For if he lays the foundation, then discovers that he is unable to finish it, then everyone who sees it will begin to ridicule him, saying, 'This man started to build but wasn't able to finish!'

Or, suppose a king intends to wage war against another king. Will he not first sit down and consider whether he is able with ten thousand men to oppose the one coming against him with twenty thousand? If he determines that he is unable to win, he will send a delegation to the other while he is still a long way off seeking peace terms. In the same way, whoever does not forsake all that he has, cannot be my disciple. Salt is good; but if the salt has lost its saltiness, how can it be made salty again? It is neither fit for the soil, nor for the dunghill; but it is thrown out. He that has ears to hear, let him pay attention.

When the tax collectors and sinners drew near to him, the scribes and Pharisees began to murmur against him saying, "This man accepts sinners and eats with them." Then Jesus told them this parable:

Which one of you, having a hundred sheep and losing one, doesn't leave the ninety-nine out in the field and go after the lost sheep until he finds it? And when he does find it, he joyfully lays it upon his shoulder, returns home and calls his friends and neighbors together saying, 'Rejoice with me, for I have found the lost sheep.' I tell you, there is more joy in heaven over one sinner that repents, then over the ninety-nine who have no need for repentance.

Suppose a woman has ten pieces of silver and loses one. Does she not light a candle, sweep the house and search diligently until she finds it? When she finds it, she calls her friends and neighbors together saying, 'Rejoice with me, for I have found the lost coin.' Likewise, I say to you that there is joy in the presence of the Angels of G-d over the one sinner that repents.

There was a certain man who had two sons. The younger one said to his father, 'Father, give me my share of the estate.' So he divided his estate between them. Soon after, the younger son gathered together all that he had and traveled to a distant country where he squandered his wealth with wild living. After he had spent all that he had, a severe famine arose in the land and he began to be in need. So he went to work for one of the citizens of that country who sent him into his fields to feed the pigs. How he longed to fill his belly with the husks that the swine ate! But, no one gave him anything.

When he finally came to his senses, he said, 'How many of my father's hired servants have food to spare, and I am starving to death! I will arise and return to my father, and say to him: Father, I have sinned against heaven and against you. I am not worthy to be called your son; make me like one of your hired servants.' So, he arose and went to his father.

While he was still a long way off, his father saw him and was filled with compassion for him. Excitedly, he ran to him, embraced him and kissed him. Then his son said, 'Father, I have sinned against heaven, and in your sight; and I am no longer worthy to be called your son.' But, his father said to his servants, 'Hurry! Bring the best robe and put it on him! Put a ring on his finger and sandals on his feet! Bring the fattened calf and kill it. Let's have a feast and celebrate! For this son of mine was dead, and now he is alive again! He was lost, but now he is found!' And they began to celebrate.

During this time, his eldest son was in the field; and when he came near to the house and heard the sound of music and dancing, he called one of the servants aside and asked him what was going on. The servant said, 'Your brother has returned; and your father has killed the fattened calf, because he has received him safe and sound.'

The older brother became angry and refused to go into the feast; therefore, his father came out and pleaded with him to join the festivities. He said to his father, 'Look, all these years I have served you, and I have never disobeyed your orders at any time: yet, you have never given me a young goat so that I could make a feast with my friends: but as soon as this son of yours comes home, after he has devoured your wealth with prostitutes, you kill the fattened calf for him!' He said to his son, 'Son, you are always with me, and everything I have is yours. It was only right that we should celebrate and be glad; for your brother was dead, and he is alive again; he was lost, and now he is found.'

There was a rich man whose steward was accused of squandering his possessions. So, he called him and said, 'What is this I am hearing about you? Give an account of your management, for you may not be a steward much longer.' Then the steward said to himself, 'What am I going to do? My Master is taking away my job. I can't dig, and I am ashamed to beg. I know what I will do, so that, when I lose my job here, the people will welcome me into their houses.' So he called in each one of his master's debtors. He asked the first, "How much do you owe my master?" "I owe him a hundred measures of oil," he replied. Then he said to him, "Take your bill, sit down quickly, and write fifty." Then the servant said to another, "How much do you owe?" And he said, "A hundred measures of wheat." Then he said, "Take your bill and write eighty". Because he had conducted himself so shrewdly, the master commended the unjust steward. For the people of this world are more shrewd in their dealings with one another than the children of light. And I say to you, use money to make friends for yourselves, so that when you fail, they will receive you into their eternal habitations.

Whoever is trustworthy with very little, can also be trusted with much more; and whoever is dishonest with a little, will also be dishonest with much. Therefore, if you have not been faithful in handling the wealth of this world, who will commit to your trust the true riches? And if you haven't been trustworthy with another man's property, who will give you property of your own? No one can serve two masters, either he will hate the one and love the other, or else, he will be devoted to the one and despise the other. You can't serve G-d and worldly riches also.

The Pharisees, who were lovers of money, began to sneer at him when they heard these things, to whom he directed these words:

You are the ones who justify yourselves in the sight of men, but G-d knows your hearts. That which is highly revered among men is detestable in the sight of G-d. The Law and the prophets were preached until John. Since then, the Kingdom of G-d is preached and everyone is trying to force his way into it by trying to justify themselves. But I tell you, that it is easier for heaven and earth to pass away than for one stroke of the pen to fail from the Law. Whosoever divorces his wife and marries another commits adultery; and whoever marries a divorced woman commits adultery.

There was a certain rich man dressed in purple and fine linen, who lived in luxury every day; and there was a certain beggar, named Lazarus, who sat by his gait every day, full of sores and longing to be filled with the crumbs that fell from the rich man's table. Even the dogs came and licked his sores. Finally, the time came when the beggar died and was carried by the angels to Abraham's bosom: and the rich man died also and was buried. In hell, where the rich man was being tormented, he lifted up his eyes and saw Abraham far off, with Lazarus sitting by his side. Then he cried out to Abraham and said, 'Father Abraham, have mercy on me, and send Lazarus to dip the tip of his finger in water, and cool my tongue, for I am tormented in this flame.' But Abraham said, 'Son, remember that in your lifetime you enjoyed the best of everything, and Lazarus endured the worst of things; but now he is comforted, and you are tormented. Besides, between us and you there is a great gulf in place: so that those who want to cross over from here to you cannot, and neither can any pass from there to here.' Then he said, "I beg you, father, send Lazarus to my father's house, for I have five brothers. Let him warn them, less they also come to this place of torment. Abraham said, 'They have Moses and the prophets; let them listen to them.' But he said, 'No, father Abraham; but if someone went to them from the dead, they will repent.' And Abraham said, 'If they will not listen to Moses and the prophets, neither will they be convinced by someone else, even if they should rise from the dead.'

It is impossible for someone not to commit an offense; woe be to that person through whom the offense comes! It would be better for him if he were cast into the sea with a millstone hung around his neck, than that he should cause one of these little ones to sin. Watch yourselves! If your brother trespasses against you, rebuke him; and if he repents, forgive him. And, if he trespasses against you seven times a day, and seven times a day turns back to you and says, 'I repent;' you must forgive him.

(The apostle said to him, "LORD, increase our faith.")

"If you had faith as small as a grain of mustard seed, you might say to this mulberry tree, 'Be plucked up by the root and cast into the sea;' and it should obey you. Which one of you, having a servant plowing or feeding the cattle, will say to him when he comes in from the field, 'Come, sit down and eat?' Instead, would you not say to him, 'Prepare my supper, and get yourself ready to wait on me until I have finished eating and drinking, and then you may eat?' Does he thank that servant because he did the things that he was commanded to do? I don't think so. So you also, when you have done all those things which you are commanded to do, say, 'We are unworthy servants; we have only done our duty.'"

Now as he made his way to Jerusalem, Jesus traveled along the border between Samaria and Galilee. As he entered one of the villages, ten lepers came toward him. Standing at a distance, they cried out in a loud voice, "Jesus, Master, have mercy on us!" When he saw them, he said, "Go, show yourselves to the priests."

As they went on their way, they were cleansed. One of them, when he saw that he was healed, turned back to Jesus, and throwing himself down at his feet, began to glorify G-d in a loud voice and to give thanks; and he was a Samaritan. Jesus asked him, "Were not all ten cleansed? Where are the other nine? Not one of the others have returned to give glory to G-d except this stranger." Then he said to the man, "Arise, and go on your way; your faith has made you well."

When the Pharisees demanded that Jesus tell them when the Kingdom of G-d was coming, he replied,

> The Kingdom of G-d does not come by way of visual demonstration. Neither can they say, 'Look here!' Or, 'Look there!' Because the Kingdom of G-d is within you." Then Jesus directed this teaching to his disciples:

The days will come when you will desire to see just one of the days of the Son of Man, and you will not see it. And when they say to you, 'See, he is here,' or, 'See, he is there,' don't go running after them. When the Son of Man comes in his day, it will be like the light which flashes and lights up the sky from one end to the other. But first, he must suffer many things, and be rejected by this generation.

Just as it was in the days of Noah, so shall it be in the days of the Son of Man. They overate, got drunk, married many wives and were given in marriage, until the day that Noah entered the ark, and the floods came and destroyed them all. It was the same in the days of Lot. They ate, drank, bought and sold, planted and built homes; but the same day that Lot left Sodom, fire and brimstone fell from heaven and destroyed them all. Even so shall it be on the day that the Son of Man is revealed.

On that day no one standing on the rooftop, having his valuables inside, should come down and take them away. Likewise, no one in the field should go back for anything. Remember Lot's wife. Whosoever tries to save his life will lose it, and whoever loses his life will preserve it. I tell you this: on that night, there will be two in one bed; one will be taken and the other left. Two women will be grinding grain together; one will be taken, the other will be left. Two men will be in the field; one will be taken and the other will be left.

"Where, LORD?" They asked. "Wherever the body is, that's where the eagles will be gathered together" Jesus replied. Then he told his disciples a parable to teach them that they should always pray and never give up:

In a certain city there was a judge who neither feared G-d, nor cared about any man. And there was a widow in that city who kept coming to him with the same plea, saying, "Vindicate me from my adversary." For a while he refused, but finally he said to himself, "even though I don't fear G-d, nor care about any man, yet, because this widow keeps bothering me, I will see that she gets justice before she wears me out by her continuous appearances before me."

Listen to what the unjust judge said! Don't you think G-d will vindicate his own elect who cry out to him day and night! Will he put them off? I tell you that he will avenge them quickly. Nevertheless, when the Son of Man comes, will he find such confidence in G-d on the earth?

(Then to those who were confident in their own righteousness, and looked down on others, he told this parable):

Two men went into the Temple to pray; one was a tax collector and the other was a Pharisee. The Pharisee stood up and prayed within himself like this, 'G-d, I thank you that I am not like other men, robbers, evildoers, adulterers, or even like this tax collector. I fast twice a week, and I give tithes of all that I possess.' But the tax collector, standing off in the distance, would not so much as lift his eyes up toward heaven, but he beat upon his breast and said, 'G-d, be merciful to me, a sinner.' I tell you that the tax collector, rather than the Pharisee went down to his house justified in the sight of G-d. For everyone who exalts himself will be humbled; and he that humbles himself will be exalted.

People brought their babies to Jesus, so that he would touch them, and when his disciples saw it, they rebuked them. But, Jesus called the children over to him and said, "Permit the children to come to me, and don't hinder them; for of such is the Kingdom of G-d. Truly, I tell you that whoever does not receive the Kingdom of G-d as a little child, will never enter into it."

Then one of the rulers asked him, "Good master, what must I do to inherit eternal life?" "Why are you calling me, 'good'?" Jesus asked. "No one is good except G-d alone. You know the commandments: do not commit adultery; do not murder; do not steal; do not bear false witness; and honor your father and mother." "I have kept all these things since I was a boy," the man said. When Jesus heard these words, he said to him, "Yet, you are lacking one thing; sell all that you have, distribute to the poor, and you will have treasure in heaven. Then come and follow me."

When he heard these words, he became very sad because he was a wealthy man. Observing his sad countenance, Jesus said, "How hard it is for the rich to enter into the Kingdom of G-d! I tell you that it is easier for a camel to go through the eye of a needle, than for a rich man to enter the Kingdom of G-d."

Those who heard this asked, "Who then can be saved?" "The things that are impossible with man are possible with G-d" Jesus replied. Then Peter said, "Look! We have left everything and followed you; therefore, what will we have?" Jesus replied:

> Truly, I say this to all of you that have followed me; in the regeneration, when the Son of Man sits on the throne of his glory, you shall also sit upon thrones judging the twelve tribes of Israel. Everyone that has forsaken houses, brothers, sisters, father, mother, wife, children and lands for my sake shall receive a hundred times more in this life, and will inherit eternal life. But, there are many that are first that will be last; and last, that will be first.
>
> For the Kingdom of Heaven is like a land owner who went out early in the morning to hire men to work in his vineyard. After he had agreed to pay them a denarius a day, he sent them into his vineyard to work. About the third hour, he went out and found others standing idle in the marketplace, to whom he said, 'You also go into my vineyard, and whatever is right, I will pay you.' And they went their way. Again he went out at the sixth and ninth hour and did likewise. About the eleventh hour he went out and found others standing around, and he said to them, 'Why have you been standing here all day long doing nothing?' 'Because no one has hired us,' they said. So, he said to them, 'You also go into my vineyard, and whatever is right, I will give it to you.'

When evening came, the landowner said to his steward, 'Call the workers and give them their wages, beginning with the last ones hired and going on to the first.' Every worker that had been hired around the eleventh hour received a denarius. So, when those who had been hired first came, they expected to receive more, but they also received a denarius. Now, when they received it, they began to murmur against the landowner, saying, 'These last have worked but one hour, and you have made them equal to us, who have borne the burden and heat of the day.'

But he answered one of them, and said, 'Friend, I'm not doing anything wrong to you. Did you not agree to work for a denarius? Take your wages and go; I want to give to these last the same as I gave to you. Is it not lawful for me to do what I want with my own money? Are you angry with me because I am generous?' So the last shall be first, and the first shall be last. Many are called, but only a few are chosen.

Now as Jesus continued his journey towards Jerusalem, he took his twelve disciples aside and said to them, "Listen, we are going up to Jerusalem; and the Son of Man will be betrayed into the hands of the chief priests and teachers of the Law. They will condemn him to death, and turn him over to the Gentiles to be mocked, beaten and crucified. But on the third day he will rise again."

Then the mother of James and John, the sons of Zebedee, came to Jesus with her two sons. She knelt before him and asked him for a favor. "What is it that you wish?" Jesus asked. "Grant that my two sons may sit on either side of you in your kingdom." She said. Jesus answered her thus, "You don't know what you are asking." Then he said to her two sons, "Are you able to drink of the cup that I will drink of, and to be baptized with the baptism that I am baptized with?" They replied, "We are able." "Indeed, you will drink of my cup, and be baptized with the baptism that I am baptized with," Jesus said. "But as for who will sit on my right and left side is not for me to determine. These seats belong to those for whom my Father has reserved them."

When the ten heard it, they were filled with indignation against the two brothers. But, Jesus called them all together and said, "You know that the rulers of the Gentiles exercise dominion over them, and their high officials exercise authority over them. Not so with you; for whoever wants to be great among you, let him be your minister; and whoever will be the chief among you, let him be your servant; just as the Son of Man did not come to be attended to, but to minister, and to give his life as a ransom for many."

As they left Jericho, a great multitude followed him. When two blind men who were sitting by the wayside heard that Jesus was passing by, they immediately began to cry out, "Have mercy upon us, O' LORD, son of David!" The crowd rebuked them and told them to be quiet, but they shouted all the louder, "LORD, son of David, have mercy on us!" Jesus stopped and called them, saying, "What do you want me to do for you?" "LORD, that our eyes may be opened," they replied. Jesus had compassion on them and touched their eyes. Instantly, they received their sight and followed him.

There was a certain chief tax collector, named Zacchaeus, who was very wealthy. He also wanted to see who Jesus was, but being a short man, he was unable to see him because of the crowds. Therefore, he ran ahead of the multitude and climbed up a sycamore tree to see him since Jesus was coming that way. When Jesus reached the place where Zacchaeus was, he looked up and said, "Zacchaeus, hurry and come down; for I must stay at your house today." Zacchaeus came down at once and welcomed him gladly. When the crowd saw this they began to murmur, "This man is going to be the guest of a sinner!" Then Zacchaeus stood before them all and said, "Look, LORD! Right here and now I give half of my assets to the poor; and if I have taken anything from anyone by a false claim, I will pay them back four times the amount." Jesus said, "Today, salvation has come to this house, for as much as he is also a son of Abraham. For the Son of Man has come to seek and to save that which was lost."

He went on to speak a parable to them because he was nearing Jerusalem, and they thought the Kingdom of G-d was imminent:

A man of noble birth went to a distant country to have himself appointed king, intending to return. So he called ten of his servants and gave them ten minas, and said, 'Trade with this until I return.' In the meantime, his subjects hated him, and sent a message to him, saying, 'We will not have this man to reign over us.' Nevertheless, he was made king and returned home. Then he called his servants, to whom he had given the money, in order to find out what they had gained by trading. The first one came and said, 'LORD, your mina has earned ten more.' And he said, 'Well done! You're a good servant! Because you've been faithful in a small matter, take authority over ten cities.' The second came and said, 'LORD, your mina has gained five minas.' And his master said, 'Take authority over five cities.' The third came and said, 'LORD, here is your mina which I have laid away in a piece of cloth; for I was afraid of you, because you're a hard man. You take up that which you didn't lay down, and reap what you didn't plant.' His master exclaimed, "I will judge you by your own words, you wicked servant! You knew from the beginning that I was a hard man, taking up what I didn't lay down, and reaping what I didn't plant. Why then did you not put my money on deposit, so that at my return I could have collected it with interest?" Then he said to those standing by, "Take the mina away from him and give it to the one who gained the ten minas." Then they said to him, 'Sir, he already has ten!' However, he said, "I tell you that to everyone who has, more will be given; but, as for the one who has nothing, even what little he has will be taken away. And those enemies of mine that didn't want me to reign over them, bring them here, and kill them in front of me."

After he spoke these words, he continued on his journey towards Jerusalem. As they walked, Jesus said to his disciples, "It is written:

> In the tenth day of this month every man, according to the size of their family, will take a male lamb, one without blemish; and you shall watch and safeguard it until the fourteenth day of this month; then the whole congregation of Israel shall kill it in the evening. You shall not let it remain until the morning, nor shall you break one of its bones; for it is the LORD's Passover.

On that day the priest will make an atonement for you, to cleanse you, that you may be clean from all your sins before the LORD. He shall make an atonement for the Sanctuary, the Tabernacle of the congregation, the altar, the priests, and for all the people in the congregation. He will consecrate you for seven days.

And on the first day, you shall take the branches of healthy palm trees and thick trees and rejoice before the LORD.

When you see these things come to pass, remember that I told you ahead of time. For the Son of Man shall surely be examined and tried, but they will find no fault in him.

XIII.

The Passover Feast was drawing closer, and at this time of year multitudes of people from every town and village in Israel went up to Jerusalem to purify themselves. Upon entering the City scores of people went to the Temple in search of Jesus, but he had not yet arrived. As they stood in the Temple waiting for him, they began to question one another, saying, "What do you think? Do you think he will come to the Feast?"

Now, both the chief priests and Pharisees had gathered the Temple guards together in the Temple and said to them, "We are asking you to go and familiarize yourselves with his hideout and take knowledge of who has seen him there. It is said that he is very subtle; therefore, find out all his hiding places and come back to us with some assurance, and we will go with you." (They did this in hopes of capturing him in some private place).

In the meantime, they sent messengers to King Herod, saying, "O king, since the desire of your heart is to come to Jerusalem, even so come. For we will deliver this Jesus into the king's hand." As soon as Herod received the message, he was overjoyed and made immediate preparation to go to Jerusalem because he wanted to meet with Jesus.

Six days before the Passover, Jesus entered the village of Bethany and went to the house of Lazarus, whom he had raised from the dead. Mary and Martha prepared a special meal for him. While Martha served, Mary went and bowed herself at the feet of Jesus and said, "Let your handmaid be a servant to wash the feet of the servants of my LORD." Then she took a pound of spikenard perfume, which was very expensive, and anointed the feet of Jesus; wiping them with her hair. Immediately, the entire room was filled with the odor of the ointment. Judas Iscariot, the one that was to betray him, objected and said, "Why was this perfume not sold for three hundred denarii and given to the poor?" (He didn't object because he cared about the poor, but because he was a thief. He was in charge of the money bag, and would help himself to what was put into it). "Leave her alone!" Jesus said. "She intended to use this on the day of my burial. You will always have the poor with you; but you will not always have me."

Meanwhile a large crowd of Jews discovered that Jesus was at Bethany and went out to see him; and not only to see him, but to see Lazarus also. Now, the chief priests had made plans to kill Lazarus along with Jesus, because many people had turned away and believed on Jesus when he raised him from the dead.

The following day, Jesus began his triumphant entry into Jerusalem accompanied by his disciples. As they approached the Mount of Olives, he sent two of his disciples ahead of him, saying, "Go to the village ahead of you. As soon as you enter, you will see a donkey tied up there with her colt beside her. Untie them and bring them to me; and if anyone says anything to you, say to them, 'The LORD needs them,' and he will send them." When they entered the village they found everything to be as he said it would be. As they were loosing the colt, the owners came out and said to them, "Why are you loosing the colt?" "The LORD needs them," the disciples replied. So, the owners let them go, just as Jesus predicted. When the disciples returned to Jesus, they threw their garments on the colt and sat him upon it. Now, when the people heard that Jesus was coming to Jerusalem, they took branches of palm trees and other trees and went out to meet him, spreading their garments along the way. As he reached the descent of the Mount of Olives, the entire multitude began to rejoice and to shout praises to G-d for all of the miraculous works they had witnessed.

"Blessed be the King that comes in the name of the LORD!" They shouted. "Peace in heaven and glory in the highest! Hosanna to the Son of David! Hosanna in the highest!" The people that followed behind him made music with pipes and rejoiced with such great joy that it felt as though the earth was shaking from the noise. Then some of the Pharisees who were among the crowd began to plead with him, "Teacher! Rebuke your disciples!" Jesus answered, "I tell you, that if these should hold their peace, the stones would immediately begin to shout." As he neared the gates of the City, Jesus began to weep. Then he raised his voice and said:

If only you knew, if at no other time then today, the things that belong to your peace! But, now they are hidden from your eyes. For the days are coming when your enemies will dig a trench around you, surround you, and prevent you from escaping on every side. They will raze the City to the ground while your children are still within its walls. They won't leave in you one stone upon another, because you didn't know the time of your visitation. Often times the LORD spoke by the mouth of the prophets, saying:"

Execute judgment and righteousness, and deliver those who have been robbed from the hand of the oppressor.

Do no wrong or violence to the strangers, the fatherless or widow, nor shed innocent blood in this place.

For if you do this thing indeed, then kings who sit on David's throne will come through these gates riding in chariots and on horses, accompanied by his servants and his people.

But if you refuse to obey these words, I swear by myself, this place will become desolate.

(All this was done in fulfillment of the words of the prophets):

He has come to the gate of my people, even Jerusalem. One who breaks open has gone before them: and their King shall pass before them, the LORD at their head.

Rejoice greatly, O daughter of Zion, and shout! Behold, your King is coming to you. He is righteous, having salvation, meek and riding upon a donkey, upon a colt, the foal of a donkey.

Cry out and shout inhabitants of Zion! For great is the Holy One of Israel in the midst of you! For the LORD of Hosts has visited his flock, the house of Judah.

Lift up your heads, O gates, and be lifted up, you ancient doors, so that the King of Glory may come in. Who is this King of Glory? The LORD strong and mighty, the LORD mighty in battle!

Lift up your heads, O gates, and be lifted up you everlasting doors, so that the King of Glory may

come in. Who is this King of Glory? The LORD of
Hosts, he is the King of Glory!

When he entered Jerusalem, the whole City was stirred; and
when several visitors asked, "Who is this?" Certain ones in
the crowd responded, "This is Jesus, the prophet of
Nazareth!" At this the Pharisees said to one another, "See,
this is getting us nowhere! How can we prevail when the
whole world is going after him?!"

Moments after entering the Temple, Jesus began to cast out
all those that bought and sold merchandise therein. He
overthrew the tables of the money changers, and the seats
of those who sold the doves. Angrily, he shouted, "It is
written, 'My house shall be called a house of prayer;' but
you have made it a den of thieves!"

After the merchants left the Temple, and all had been set in
place, the blind and the lame came to him, and he healed
them. When the chief priests and scribes saw the miracles
that he did, and the people crying out in the Temple,
"Hosanna to the Son of David," they were greatly displeased
and desperately wanted to destroy him. "Do you hear what
they're saying?" They asked him. "Yes," Jesus replied. "Have
you never read, 'Out of the mouth of babes and sucklings,
you have perfected praise?'" When he left there, he
returned to Bethany, where he lodged with the twelve.

In the morning, as he was returning to the City, he began to
be hungry. Seeing a fig tree by the road, he went up to it,
but found nothing but leaves. Then he said to the tree, "Let
no fruit grow on you, hereafter or forever." Immediately the
fig tree began to wither. When the disciples saw it, they
were awestruck, saying, "Look how quickly the fig tree
withered away!"

"Have faith in G-d," Jesus replied. "For truly I say to you that if you have faith and do not doubt, you will not only do what was done to the fig tree, but if you say to this mountain, 'Go, throw yourself into the sea,' it will be done. Therefore, I tell you that if you believe, you will receive whatever you ask for in prayer." Soon after, they entered the Temple and Jesus sat down to teach.

As he was teaching, the chief priests and elders of the people came to him and said, "By what authority do you do these things, and who gave you this authority?" Jesus replied, "I will also ask you one thing, and if you can answer it, I will tell you by what authority I do these things. The baptism of John – where did it come from? Did it come from heaven, or from man?" Then they began to reason among themselves and said, "If we say, 'From heaven,' he will ask, 'Why didn't you believe him then?' But, if we say, 'From men,' then we fear the reaction of the people because they all regard John to be a prophet." So, after careful deliberation they answered him, "We can't tell." "Neither can I tell you by what authority I do these things," Jesus replied.

Then he said to them, Tell me what you think.

" A certain man had two sons. He went to the first and said, 'Son, go to work today in my vineyard.' The son answered, 'I will not,' but afterward he repented and went. Then he went to the second and said the same thing. And his son answered, 'I will go, sir,' but he never went. Which one of the two did his father's will?" "The first one," they answered. "Most assuredly, I tell you that the tax collectors and the prostitutes will go into the Kingdom of G-d before you! For John came to you in order to show you the way of righteousness, and you didn't believe him, but the tax collectors and prostitutes did. They repented; you never did!"

Hear another parable: There was a certain householder who planted a vineyard. He planted hedges all around, dug a winepress in it, built a tower and leased it out to farmers, and went away on a journey. As the month of harvest drew near, he sent his servants to the farmers to collect some of the fruit. The farmers seized his servants, beat one, killed another, and stoned a third. Once again, he sent more of his servants to them and they treated them the same way. Finally, he sent his son to them saying, 'They will respect my son.' But when they saw the son, they reasoned among themselves, saying, 'This is the heir, let us kill him and seize his inheritance.' They captured him, cast him out of the vineyard and killed him. Therefore, when the LORD of the vineyard comes, what will he do to those farmers?

The chief priests said to him, "He will destroy those wicked men and lease out his vineyard to other farmers who will give him his share of the crop at harvest time." Jesus asked, "Have you never read these words in the Scriptures? The stone which the builders rejected, the same has become the chief corner stone; this is the LORD's doing and is marvelous in our eyes? Therefore, I say to you that the Kingdom of G-d shall be taken away from you and given to a people that will produce its fruit. And I will tell you something else; whosoever falls upon this stone will be broken to pieces, but the one on whom it falls, will surely be ground to powder." When the chief priests and Pharisees heard this parable, they perceived that he was speaking of them. They desperately wanted to seize him, but were afraid of the people, because they took him to be a prophet. Then Jesus continued his teaching:

> The Kingdom of Heaven is likened to a certain King who prepared a wedding banquet for his son. He sent his servants to those who had been invited to the wedding to tell them to come, but they refused. Then he sent other servants to them, saying, 'I have prepared my dinner: My oxen and fattened cattle have been killed and everything is ready: come to the wedding.' But they made light of it and went on their way, one to his field and another to his merchandise. The rest of them seized his servants, mistreated them and some they killed. When the king heard of it, he was enraged; and in his fury, he sent forth his army, destroyed those murderers and burned their city. Then he said to his servants, 'The wedding is ready, but those who were invited aren't worthy. Therefore, go into the streets and invite everyone to the wedding that you can find.' So the servants went into the streets and gathered all the people they could find, both good and bad, and the wedding was filled with guests. When the king came in to see the guests, he noticed a man who did not have on a wedding garment. 'Friend,' he asked, 'How did you get in here without a wedding garment?' And the man was speechless. Therefore, the king said to his servants, 'Bind him hand and foot, and cast him out into utter darkness, where there will be weeping and gnashing of teeth.' Many are invited, but few are chosen.

As Jesus was teaching, certain disciples of the Pharisees and the Herodians entered the Temple. Their objective was to try and confound him and trap him in his words. "Teacher," they said. "We know that you are a man of virtue and teach the way of G-d in truth. Neither are you swayed by a man's position, because you have no regard for the titles of men. Tell us therefore, what do you think? Is it lawful to give tribute to Caesar or not?" Perceiving their wickedness, he answered, "Why do you tempt me, you hypocrites? Show me the tribute money!" When they handed him a denarius, he asked them, "Whose image and superscription is on this coin?" "Caesar's," they replied. Then he said, "Give to Caesar the things that belong to Caesar, and give to G-d the things that belong to G-d." When they heard these words, they marveled and left the Temple.

But certain Sadducees, a sect which did not believe in the resurrection, came forward to ask him a question. "Teacher," they asked, "Moses told us that if a man dies without having children, his brother must marry the widow and have children for him. Now, there were seven brothers. The first one married and died, and since he had no children, he left her to his brother. Likewise, the same thing happened to the second and third brother, right on down to the seventh. Finally, the woman died also. Therefore, in the resurrection, whose wife will she be of the seven, since she was married to them all?" "You are in error," Jesus said. "For you neither know the Scriptures nor the power of G-d. In the resurrection, they neither marry, nor are they given in marriage, but they are like the Angels of G-d in heaven. But, touching on the resurrection of the dead, have you never read what G-d said to Moses in the bush, 'I am the G-d of Abraham, the G-d of Isaac, and the G-d of Jacob'? G-d is the G-d of the living, not of the dead."

When the multitude heard these words, they marveled at his doctrine. But, when the Pharisees heard that Jesus had put them to silence, they gathered together against him. One of them, an expert in the Law, tested him with this question: "Teacher, which is the greatest commandment in the Law?" "The foremost and greatest of all the commandments is this," Jesus responded. "Hear, O Israel, the LORD our G-d is one LORD; and you shall love the LORD your G-d with all your heart, and with all your soul and with all your mind. And, the second one is like the first, 'you shall love your neighbor as yourself.' On these two commandments hang all the Law and the Prophets."

Turning to the Pharisees, Jesus asked, "What do you think of the Messiah? Whose son is he?" "The son of David," they replied. Then he said, "Why then does David, speaking in the spirit, call him 'LORD'? For he says, 'The LORD said to my LORD sit on my right hand, till I make your enemies your footstool.' If David calls him 'LORD,' how can he be his son?" None of them were able to answer him a single word; and having been put to shame before the people, they walked out of the Temple. From that day on they didn't dare ask him any more questions. As they were leaving, Jesus addressed his followers:

The teachers of the Law and the Pharisees sit in Moses' seat. Therefore, whatever they tell you that you must observe and do, do it. But, do not do the things they do, for they don't practice the things they teach. They tie up heavy burdens, much too heavy to carry, and lay them upon men's shoulders, but they are unwilling to lift one of their fingers to move them. Everything they do, they do to be noticed, including broadening their phylacteries and enlarging the tassels on their garments. They love to sit in the place of honor at feasts and in the chief seats in the synagogue; and they love to be greeted in the marketplace, and have people call them, 'Rabbi.' But you are not to be called 'Rabbi,' for you have only one Master, the Messiah, and all of you are brothers. Don't call anyone 'Father,' upon the earth either, for you have only one Father, and he is in heaven. Nor are you to be called 'Teacher,' for you have one teacher, the Christ. He that is the greatest among you will be your servant. For whoever exalts himself will be humbled, and whoever humbles himself will be exalted.

(As he was teaching, several of the Pharisees and doctors of the Law entered the Temple, whom Jesus began to rebuke):

> Woe be to you scribes and Pharisees, hypocrites! For you shut the Kingdom of Heaven up in men's faces. You will not enter in yourselves, neither will you allow those who want to enter the Kingdom to go in!

> Woe to you scribes and Pharisees, hypocrites! You devour the houses of widows, and for a show make lengthy prayers. Therefore, you will surely receive the greater damnation!

> Woe to you scribes and Pharisees, hypocrites! You travel over land and see to win a single convert, and when he converts, you make him twice as much the child of hell than yourselves!

> Woe to you blind guides! You say, 'If anyone swears by the Temple, it means nothing; but if anyone swears by the gold of the Temple, he is bound by his oath!' You blind fools! Which is greater: the gold, or the Temple that makes the gold sacred!? You blind fools!

Which is greater: the gift, or the altar that makes the gift sacred? Whoever swears by the altar, swears by it and everything that is on it; and he that swears by the Temple, swears by it and by the One who dwells in it; and he that swears by heaven, swears by G-d's throne and by him that sits on it!

Woe to you scribes and Pharisees, hypocrites! You pay tithes of mint, dill and cumin, and have omitted the most important matters of the Law – judgment, mercy, and faith! These you should have done without leaving the other undone. You blind guides! You strain at a gnat and swallow a camel!

Woe to you scribes and Pharisees, hypocrites! You make the outside of the cup and the platter clean, but their insides are full of greed and extortion! Blind Pharisees! Cleanse the inside of the cup and platter first, and the outside will also be clean!

Woe to you scribes and Pharisees, hypocrites! You are like whitewashed tombs, which look beautiful on the outside, but within you are full of dead men's bones and filth! In the same way, outwardly you appear to be righteous before men, but on the inside you are full of hypocrisy and iniquity!

Woe to you scribes and Pharisees, hypocrites! You build the tombs of the prophets and decorate the graves of the righteous, and then you say, 'If we had lived during the days of our forefathers, we wouldn't have taken part in shedding the blood of the prophets.' Whereas you are witnesses against yourselves that you are the descendants of them who killed the prophets. Fill up, then, the measure of your forefathers' sin!

You snakes! You brood of vipers! How can you escape the damnation of hell?! I am sending you prophets, wise men and teachers. Some of them you will kill and crucify, and others you will flog in your synagogues and pursue them from town to town. Therefore, all of the righteous blood that has been shed on the earth will come upon you; from the blood of righteous Abel, to the blood of Zechariah, the son of Berechiah, whom you murdered between the Temple and the altar. Truly I say to you, all this will come upon this generation.

(Lifting his eyes from the people, he stretched out his hands toward heaven, saying):

O' Jerusalem, Jerusalem, you who killed the prophets and stone those who are sent to you, how often I have longed to gather your children together, even as a hen gathers her chicks under her wings, but you would have no part of me! Look how your house is left to you, desolate! For I say to you that you will not see me from here on until you say, 'Blessed is he who comes in the name of the LORD.'

As he was departing the Temple, he noticed the rich casting their gifts into the treasury. When he saw a certain widow casting in two very small coins, he turned to his disciples and commented: "Truthfully I tell you, this poor widow has cast in more than all of them. For they have given an offering to G-d out of their excess; but she, in her poverty, has cast in all that she had." After he said these things he left the Temple.

When his disciples began to point out to him how the Temple was adorned with beautiful stones and other gifts dedicated to G-d, Jesus remarked, "Take a good look at these great buildings. For the time is coming when there won't be one stone left upon another; every one of them will be thrown down."

Then Philip and Andrew told Jesus that there were some Greeks who had come to Jerusalem for the Passover, and that they wanted to see him. Jesus said, "The time has come for the Son of Man to be glorified. Most assuredly, I tell you, except a kernel of wheat falls into the ground and dies, it remains a single seed. But if it dies, it produces many seeds. Remember, he that loves his life will lose it; and he that hates his life in this world will live eternally. If anyone wishes to serve me, he must follow me; and where I am, that is where my servant will be also. If any man wants to serve me, my Father will honor him. Right now my heart is troubled, and what can I say? 'Father, save me from this hour?' No, it was for this very reason that I came to this hour." Looking up towards heaven, Jesus said, "Father, glorify your name!" Then a voice came from heaven saying, "I have both glorified it, and I will glorify it again." Some in the crowd said, "It thundered!" Others said, "An angel spoke to him!" Then Jesus said, "This voice didn't come for my benefit, but for yours. Now is the time for judgment on this world: now will the Prince of this world be driven out! And, if I am lifted up from the earth, I will draw all men to myself." He said these words with his arms stretched out, demonstrating how he would die.

Immediately, an unbeliever spoke up in the crowd, "We have heard from the Law that the Messiah will live forever, so how can you say, 'The Son of Man must be lifted up?' Who is this 'Son of Man'?" Then Jesus told them, "The Light will be with you a little while longer. Walk while you have the Light, before darkness overpowers you. The man who walks in the dark doesn't know where he is going. While you have the Light, believe in the Light, so that you may become the children of Light."

Shouting aloud for all to hear, Jesus cried out, "He that believes on me, not only believes on me, but on the One who sent me! When he looks at me, he sees the One who sent me. I have come to be a light in the world, so that whosoever believes on me should not remain in the darkness. If any man hears my words and does not believe in me, I don't judge him. I didn't come to judge the world, but to save the world. He that rejects me and refuses to accept my words has a judge; the word that I have spoken, the same will condemn him at the last day. For I haven't spoken of my own accord, but the Father who sent me gave me a commandment as to what I should say and how to say it. And I know that his commandment leads to everlasting life. Therefore, I speak as the Father commands me to." After he said these things, he continued on his way to the Mount of Olives where he remained all night in prayer.

XIV.

As Jesus sat upon the Mount of Olives early in the morning, his disciples came to him and asked, "LORD, tell us when these things will come to pass. What will be the sign of your coming, and of the end of the world?" Then Jesus answered:

Woe be to you, whoever he may be, that desires the day of the LORD! What will the end mean to you? Do you think that day will be a day of joy and happiness? No; I tell you, that day will be a day of sorrow, misery and pain; it is the day of the LORD's vengeance, and the year of retribution to uphold the controversy of Zion. Besides, do you think it is the work of righteousness to rejoice when your enemy falls; or to be glad when he stumbles? Remember this; the LORD has no delight in the death of the wicked. This is the plan that is purposed upon the whole earth: and this is the hand that is stretched out upon all the nations. Listen to what the LORD has said regarding that day:"

Come near, all you nations, to listen! Listen very carefully, all of you people in the earth!

> Proclaim this among the Gentiles: Prepare war! Wake up your mighty men, and let all the soldiers draw near and advance.

> Beat your plowshares into swords, and your pruning hooks into spears. Let the heathen be awakened and come up to the Valley of Jehoshaphat: for in that place will I sit to judge all the unbelievers. For the indignation of the LORD

will be upon all nations, and my fury will be upon all your armies!

In that day you will be utterly destroyed and given to the slaughter! And those that are slain of the LORD in that day shall be everywhere, from one end of the earth to the other. No one will mourn for them, gather them up, nor bury them, but they shall be as manure upon the ground.

Wail and howl! For the day of the LORD is near! It will be a day of destruction from the Almighty.

Because of this, all hands will go limp and every man's heart will melt. Terror will seize them; pain and anguish will grip them, and they will be in pain like a woman in labor. When the day of the LORD comes, he will destroy all the sinners that are in it.

I revealed myself to those who did not ask for me; I was found by those that never looked for me. I said, "Here am I, here am I," to a nation that was not called by my name.

I have spread out my hands all day long to a defiant people, to a people that walks in a way that is not good, who run after their own imaginations; to a people that provoke me to anger continuously to my face; that sacrifice in gardens, and burn incense upon altars of brick; to a people who say, 'Stand by yourself, keep away! Do not come near me; for I am holier than you.'

These are a smoke in my nose, a fire that burns all day. Therefore, will I destine you to the sword, and you will all bow down to the slaughter; because when I called, you did not answer, and when I spoke, you did not listen, but continued to practice evil before my eyes, and to choose that which displeased me.

Yes, in that day you will go into the holes of the rocks, and into the caves of the earth, for fear of the LORD, and for the glory of his Majesty, when I arise to shake the earth with great force.

The day of the LORD is near upon all the heathen: as you have done, it shall be done to you; your reward will return upon your own head.

Fear, the pit, and the trap, are upon you, O' inhabitant of the earth! And it shall come to pass, that he who flees from the noise of the terror shall fall into the pit; and he that comes up out of the midst of the pit shall be caught in the trap!

For the Windows from on high are open, and the foundations of the earth will shake. I will punish all the world for their evil, and the wicked for their iniquities; and I will cause the arrogance of the proud to cease and humble the pride of the ruthless.

Woe to you that call evil good, and good evil; that put darkness for light, and light for darkness; that change bitter into sweet, and sweet into bitter!

Woe to you that are wise in your own eyes, and prudent in your own sight!

Woe to them that are mighty to drink wine, and are champions at mixing drinks!

Woe to you who justify the wicked for reward, and take away the righteousness of the righteous from him!

Therefore, as the fire devours the stubble, and the flame consumes the chaff, so their root shall be rotten, and their blossom shall go up as dust, because they have cast away the Law of the LORD *of Hosts and despised the word of the Holy One of Israel.*

Therefore, I will cause the heavens to shake, and the earth will be moved out of her place. In the day of the wrath and anger of the LORD of Hosts, the earth will rock back and forth like a drunkard, and will be removed like the cottage; and because the transgression thereof will be heavy upon it, it will fall, and never rise again.

At that day the heavens will be rolled together as a scroll: and all their host will fall down, as a leaf falls off the vine, and as a falling fig from the fig tree.

For all the stars in the heavens and their constellations will not give their light: the sun will be dark when it rises, and the moon will not cause her light to shine, and all the host of heaven will be dissolved. For my sword will be bathed in heaven: and it will come down upon Idumea and the people of my curse, for judgment.

Be aware; that no man deceives you. For many shall come in my name, preaching that I am the Christ, and will deceive many. Don't be like those against whom it is written:

Son of Man, prophesy against the shepherds of Israel: prophesy, and say to them, this is what the LORD has said to the shepherds;

Woe be to the shepherds of Israel that feed themselves! Should the shepherds not feed the flocks?

Behold! I am against the shepherds: I will require my flock at their hands, and cause them to cease from feeding the flock; neither will the shepherds feed themselves anymore; for I will deliver my flock from their mouth, that they may not be food for them.

Look, I will search for my sheep, and seek them out. I will bring them out from the people, and gather them from all the countries where they have been scattered, and will bring them to their own land, and feed them upon the mountains of Israel by the rivers, and in all the inhabited places of the country.

I will seek those who are lost, and bring back those who were driven away. I will bind up those that were injured, and strengthen the sick; but the fat and the strong I will destroy. I will feed them with judgment.

O Woe be to the foolish prophets, that follow their own spirit, and have seen nothing! Their visions are false and their divinations a lie.

They say, 'the LORD has said,' when the LORD has not sent them; yet they expect their words to be confirmed, and have made others to hope that their words would be confirmed.

But, if they had stood in my counsel, and had caused my people to hear my words, then they would have turned them from their evil ways, and from the evil of their doings.

Concerning the Law and the testimony: if they do not speak in accordance with this word, it is because there is no light in them.

When you hear of wars and rumors of wars, see that you are not troubled: for all these things must come to pass, but the end is still to come. For nation shall rise up against nation, and kingdom shall stand against kingdom: and in various places there will be famines, epidemics, and earthquakes. In the heavens there will be great signs and fearful sights in the sun, moon and stars. But all these things are just the beginning of sorrows.

They will deliver you up to be afflicted, and many of you will be put to death. But before that, they will strike you with their hands and persecute you. They will bring you before the synagogues and cast you into prison, and you will be hated by all nations for my name's sake.

In that day every one that is found shall be thrust through with the sword. Your children will be dashed to pieces before your eyes; your house is spoiled, and your wives ravished. Your young men will be cut to pieces; and they will have no pity on the children.

They will turn to you for a testimony. Therefore, settle it in your hearts not to meditate beforehand how you will answer them; for I will give you the words and wisdom that none of your adversaries will be able to resist or contradict.

At that time many of your people will turn away from the faith, and will hate and betray one another. They will be betrayed by parents, brothers, sisters, relatives and friends; and some of them they will cause to be put to death. Yes, you will be hated by all men because of me; and because iniquity shall abound, the love of many will grow cold; but he that endures to the end will be saved. When you see Jerusalem surrounded by armies, then know that its desolation is near.

When you see the abomination of desolation, spoken of by Daniel the prophet, standing in the holy place, then let them which are in Judea flee into the mountains. Don't let him who is on the house top come down to take anything out of his house; neither let him who is in the field return back to take his clothes. For these are the days of vengeance when all things that are written must be fulfilled. These are the days when great distress and wrath will be upon the land and upon the people because of their unbelief; the time when many of them will be taken captive and brought into other nations.

In that day great pain and anguish will be upon those that are with child and upon them that breast-feed. Therefore, pray that your flight is not in the winter, neither on the Sabbath day. For at that time there will be great tribulation, such as has never been since the beginning of the world to this time; no, nor ever shall be. And except those days are shortened, there would be no flesh saved; but for the elect's sake those days will be shortened. And, as it is written:

It shall come to pass in that day, that I will destroy all the nations that come against Jerusalem. And I will pour upon the house of David, and upon the inhabitants of Jerusalem, the Spirit of grace and of supplications: and they will look upon me, the one whom they have pierced, and they will mourn, as one mourns for his only son, and grieve bitterly, as one that grieves for his firstborn.

Then if any man says, 'Look, here is Christ,' or, 'He is over there;' don't believe it. For there will arise false

Christs, and false prophets, that will show magnificent signs and wonders; so overwhelming, that if it were possible, they will deceive the very elect.

Look, I am telling you before it happens. Therefore, if they say to you, 'Look, he is in the desert!' Don't go. Or, 'Look, he is in the secret chambers!' Don't believe it. For as the lightning comes out of the east, and shines even to the West; so shall also the coming of the Son of Man be. For wherever the carcass is, that is where the Eagles will be gathered together. That day is indeed, a day of wrath, a day of anguish and distress, a day of ruin and desolation, a day of darkness and gloom, a day of clouds and thick blackness, a day when the trumpet sounds an alarm against the fenced cities, and against the high towers. For great distress will be upon all men, and they will walk around as though they were blind, because they have been rebellious against the LORD. Again, it is written:

In the day of my wrath neither their silver nor their gold will be able to deliver them; but the whole world will be devoured by the fire of my jealousy: for a speedy riddance will be made of all sinners that dwell in the land.

Immediately after the tribulation of those days the sun will be darkened; the moon will not shine her light; the stars will fall from heaven; and the powers of the heavens will be shaken. Then the sign of the Son of Man will appear in heaven; and when they see the Son of Man coming in the clouds of heaven with power and great glory, all the people of the earth will begin to mourn. At that time, he will send his angels with a great blast of the trumpet, and they will gather together his elect from the four winds, from one end of heaven to the other. And they will no longer be a prey to the heathen or to the beast of the field, but they will dwell in safety, and nothing will ever frighten them again.

Now learn a lesson from the fig tree; when its branch is yet tender, and sheds its leaves, you know that summer is near. Even so, when you see all these things, know that the day of the LORD is near, right at the doors. Truly, I say unto you, this generation shall not pass away until all these things are fulfilled.

After this gospel of the kingdom is preached throughout the world for a witness to every nation, then shall the end come; for heaven and earth will pass away, but my words will never pass away. No one knows when that day and hour will come; no, not even the angels of heaven, but my Father only. But as it was in the days of Noah, so shall also the coming of the Son of Man be. For in the days before the flood they were eating and drinking, marrying and giving one another in marriage, until the day that Noah entered into the ark. They didn't believe what was going to happen until the flood came, and took them all away; so shall also the coming of the Son of Man be.

In that day, two will be in the field; one will be taken, and the other left. Two women will be grinding at the mill; one will be taken, and the other left. Therefore, keep watch, because you don't know what hour your LORD is coming. But know this, that if the good man of the house had known in what watch the thief was coming, he would have watched, and would not have allowed his house to be broken into. Therefore, be ready: for the Son of Man will come at a time when you don't expect him.

Who then is a faithful and wise servant, whom his master has made overseer over his household to give them their food at the proper time? That servant will be blessed when his master returns and finds him fulfilling his responsibilities. Truly, I say to you, he will make him an overseer over all his goods. But if that servant thinks evil in his heart and says, 'My master delays his coming,' and begins to strike his fellow servants, and to eat and drink with the drunkards; the master of that servant will come in a day when he is not looking for him, and at an hour that he is not aware of, and will cut him to pieces, and assign him a place with the hypocrites where there will be weeping and gnashing of teeth.

At that time the Kingdom of Heaven will be compared to ten virgins, who took their lamps, and went out to meet the bridegroom. Five of them were wise, and five were foolish. The foolish ones took their lamps, but took no oil with them: but the wise took vessels of oil along with their lamps. While the bridegroom tarried, they all became drowsy and fell asleep. At midnight there was a cry made, 'Look, the bridegroom is coming! Let us go out to meet him!' All the virgins arose, and trimmed their lamps. Then the foolish ones said to the wise, 'Give us some of your oil, for our lamps are going out.' But the wise answered, saying, 'No; there may not be enough for us and you. Instead, go to them that sell oil, and buy some for yourselves.' And while they went to buy, the bridegroom arrived; and they that were ready went in with him to the marriage, and the door was shut. Afterward the other virgins arrived and said, 'LORD, LORD, open the door for us.' But he answered and said, 'Truly, I tell you, I don't know you.' Therefore, watch; for you don't know the day nor the hour in which the Son of Man is coming.

For the kingdom of heaven is like a man going on a journey to a far country, who called his own servants and entrusted his goods to them. To one he gave five talents, to another two, and to another one; to each servant he gave according to his various abilities; and then he took his journey. The one who had received the five talents went and traded with them and gained five more talents. Likewise, he that had received two, he also gained another two. But he that had received one talent went and dug in the earth, and hid his master's money.

After a long time, the master of those servants returned and settled accounts with them. He that had received five talents came and brought the other five talents, saying, 'Master, you gave me five talents. Look, I have gained five talents more.' His master said unto him, 'Well done! You have been a good and faithful servant. Since you have been faithful over a few things, I will put you in charge of many things.

Come and share the joy of your master.' The one who had received the two talents also came and said, 'Master, you gave me two talents. See, I have gained another two talents.' And his master said unto him, 'Well done! You're a good and faithful servant. Since you have been faithful over a few things, I will put you in charge of many things. Come and share the joy of your master.' Then he which had received the one talent came and said, 'Master, I knew that you were a hard man, reaping where you haven't sewn, and gathering where you haven't seeded. So I was afraid, and went and hid your talent in the earth. Look, here is what belongs to you.' His master said to him, 'You wicked and lazy servant! You knew that I reap where I didn't plant, and gather where I haven't seeded! Therefore, you should have put my money on deposit with the bankers, and then when I returned I would have received it back with interest.' Turning to his servants he said, 'Take the talent from him, and give it to him who has the ten talents. To those who have, more will be given, and he will have an abundance: but as for him that has nothing, even that which he has will be taken away: and cast this unprofitable servant into outer darkness, where there will be weeping and gnashing of teeth.

When the Son of Man comes in his glory, with all the holy angels with him, then he will sit upon his throne in heavenly glory. Before him will be gathered all nations: and he will separate them one from another, as a shepherd divides his sheep from the goats. And he will set the sheep on his right hand, and the goats on the left. Then shall the King say to them on his right hand, "Come, you blessed of my Father, and inherit the kingdom that has been prepared for you since the foundation of the world. For I was hungry, and you fed me: I was thirsty, and you gave me a drink: I was a stranger, and you took me in: Naked, and you clothed me: I was sick, and you visited me: I was in prison, and you came to me."

Then shall the righteous answer him, saying, "LORD, when did we see you hungry, and feed you; or thirsty, and give you a drink? When did we see you a stranger, and take you in; or naked, and clothe you? When did we see you sick, or in prison, and come to you?" And the King will answer and say unto them, "Truly, I say to you, in as much as you have done it to one of the least of these, my brethren, you have done it to me."

Then he will say to those on his left hand, "Depart from me, you cursed, into everlasting fire, prepared for the devil and his angels. For I was hungry, and you gave me no food: I was thirsty, and you gave me nothing to drink: I was a stranger, and you didn't take me in: naked, and you didn't clothe me: sick, and in prison, and you didn't visit me." Then shall they also answer him, saying, "LORD, when did we see you hungry, or thirsty, or a stranger, or naked, or sick, or in prison, and didn't minister to you?" Then he will answer them this way, "Truly I say to you, inasmuch as you didn't do it to one of the least of these, you didn't do it to me." And these will go away into everlasting punishment, but the righteous to eternal life.

Meanwhile, the chief priests, scribes and elders of the people were gathered together at the palace of Caiaphas, the high priest, consulting with one another how they might capture him by subtlety and kill him. But they decided that the Feast day would be an inopportune time; for they said, "not on the Feast day, lest there be an uproar among the people."

XV.

When Jesus had finished his teaching, he said, "You know that the Passover Feast begins in two days, and that the Son of Man will be handed over to be crucified. But I want you to know this: it is G-d who is stripping me of my glory and taking the crown from my head, no one else. Abide with me and don't be afraid. Even though the ones who are seeking my life are seeking yours also, don't be afraid; with me, you will be safe: come." Then they went to Bethany and lodged at the house of Simon, the leper.

As Jesus reclined to eat, there came in a woman having a box of expensive perfume. As she poured it on his head the disciples began to murmur against her, saying, "Why did she waste this perfume? It might have been sold for over three hundred denarii and given to the poor!" "Leave her alone." Jesus interjected. "Why are you bothering her? She has done a beautiful thing to me. The poor are always with you, but I won't be. When she poured this perfume on my body, she was unaware that she did it to prepare me for burial. Therefore, I say to you that wherever this gospel is preached throughout the whole world, what this woman has done to me will also be told for a memorial of her."

After the meal, Judas Iscariot left the house and went to the chief priests. "What will you give me," he asked, "if I deliver him to you?" After a time of bargaining, they agreed to give him thirty pieces of silver if he would deliver Jesus to them without causing a commotion to stir up the people. Then

Judas went out and looked for an opportunity to betray him. After he had fulfilled his task, they gave him thirty pieces of silver, thus fulfilling the prophecy of Zechariah:

> I said to them, 'if you think it is good, give me my hire, and if not, keep it.' So they weighed for my price thirty pieces of silver.

That night Jesus went to the Mount of Olives. As he prayed, he began to weep and to sigh in the bitterness of his soul:

> Be exalted, O G-d above the heavens, and let your glory be above all the earth. O' G-d, who is like you; and who can be compared to you? Your righteousness reaches far beyond the skies! My soul is very heavy, because those who seek my life have set their traps and are conspiring against me; devising ways to hurt me. All day long they talk of my ruin and plot ways to deceive me. They have tracked me down like a lion hungry for prey, like a great lion crouching in cover. They have prepared a net for my steps. They have dug a pit for me, which they have fallen into themselves.
>
> Yes, even my close friend, whom I accepted, and who ate my bread, has lifted up his heel against me. But, I know that my witness is in heaven and my record is on high. With my lips have I declared all the judgments of your mouth, and I have rejoiced in your testimony. When I look upon the transgressors, I am grieved because they don't keep your word. My eyes pour out tears to my G-d; rivers of waters run out from my eyes because they refuse to keep your Law.

I have become a stranger to my brothers, an alien to my mother's children; yes, even the small children despised me and spoke evil against me. Nevertheless, my mouth will declare your salvation and your righteousness all day long. Though you have made me see many sore and bitter troubles, yet, you will make me alive again and bring me up from the depths of the earth. I know that you will not leave my soul in hell; neither will you allow your Holy One to see corruption.

As for those whom you have given me, don't let them be put to shame because of me O' G-d; rather, let their reproach and shame be upon me. Show your marvelous love and kindness to them who put their trust in you, and deliver them from those who will rise up against them. How great is your goodness, which you have stored up for those who fear you, and which you bestow in the sight of men on those who take refuge in you. Your love, O LORD, reaches to the heavens, and your faithfulness to the skies. Your righteousness is likened to the mighty mountains, and your justice is compared to the great deep. How priceless is your unfailing love! Both high and low among men find refuge in the shadow of your wings; for the fountain of life is with you.

Then came the Feast of unleavened bread when the Passover must be killed. On that day, Jesus sent for Peter and John and said to them, "Go; and make preparations for us to eat the Passover." Peter asked, "Where do you want us to prepare it?" "As soon as you enter the City," Jesus replied, "you will see a man carrying a pitcher of water.

Follow him to the house that he enters, and say to the owner of the house, 'The Teacher asks: "Where is the guests' chamber where I may eat the Passover with my disciples?' He will show you a large upper room, completely furnished. Prepare it there."

When they entered the City, they found everything to be as he said it would be; and they prepared the Passover. When everything was ready, Jesus entered the upper chamber with the rest of his disciples saying, "Come, eat of my bread and drink of the wine that I have mixed."

Seating them into rows, six on either side of him, he said, "With great passion have I desired to eat this Passover with you before I suffer. For I tell you that I will not eat it again until it is fulfilled in the Kingdom of G-d." Lifting up the cup of wine, he gave thanks, and said, "Take this and divide it among yourselves: for I say to you that I will not drink of the fruit of the vine until the Kingdom of G-d comes." Then he lifted up the unleavened bread, blessed it, gave thanks, and said, "This is my body which is given for you: do this in remembrance of me."

Likewise, he took the cup after supper, and as he passed it to his disciples, he said, "Drink all of it. For this is my blood of the new covenant which is poured out for many for the remission of sins." You know that we, who are believers, all drink four cups of wine at the Passover which represent redemption, deliverance, salvation and life. But unknown to the unbelievers, they have four cups to drink as well, the cups of fury, fear and trembling, desolation, and indignation and death. Tonight, I will drink three of these cups and tomorrow I will drink the last cup, the cup of indignation and death. You may ask why I must do this and I will tell you that

I must take the judgments and curses of the Law upon myself so that whosoever will believe in me should not perish under the Law but have eternal life. This is why I have been sent. The hand of him who is going to betray me is with mine on the table. The Son of Man will go as it has been determined, but woe to that man by whom he is betrayed."

They began to inquire among themselves as to which one would do this thing. As Judas Iscariot stretched out his hand to dip his bread in the dish, Jesus said, "He that dips his hand with me in the bowl will betray me." Nervously, Judas withdrew his hand and asked, "Teacher, it is I?" "You have so answered yourself," Jesus replied.

The conversation over who would betray him resulted in a dispute over who was the greatest among them. Therefore, Jesus intervened saying, "The kings of the Gentiles lord over them, and those who exercise authority upon them are often called benefactors. But you are not to do what they do. Instead, let him who has been with me the longest, be like the one who has been with me the least amount of time; and the one who rules like the one who serves. For who is greater, the one who is at the table, or the one who serves? Is it not the one who is sitting at the table? Yet, when I am among you, I am as one who serves. You are the ones who have continued with me in my trials. I have granted you a kingdom, even as my Father has appointed one to me, so that you may eat and drink at my table in my kingdom, and sit on thrones judging the twelve tribes of Israel."

"Simon, Simon! Listen: Satan has desired to have you so that he may sift you as wheat. But I have prayed for you, Simon, that your faith does not fail. When you are converted, strengthen your brethren." Simon said, "LORD, I am ready both to go to prison with you and to die." "I will tell you this, Peter," Jesus replied, "before the rooster crows today you will deny that you know me, three times." Then Jesus asked them, "When I sent you without purse, bag or sandals, did you lack anything?" "No, nothing at all," they said. "But now," Jesus said, "he that has a purse, let him take it along with his bag; and if you do not have a sword, sell your cloak and buy one. For I tell you that this Scripture must yet be fulfilled in me, *'He was reckoned among the transgressors'*. For the things concerning me are being fulfilled." Then his disciples said, "Look LORD! Here are two swords!" "That is enough," Jesus said.

Supper being ended, Jesus arose from the table, removed his garments, took a towel, and wrapped it around his waist. They all watched with increased interest and amazement as he poured water in a basin and began to wash their feet and dry them with the towel that was around his waist. When he came to Simon Peter, Peter said to him, "LORD, you're going to wash my feet?" Jesus said, "What I am doing, you don't understand now; but you will know hereafter." Peter turned his body away from him and said, "You will never wash my feet!" "If I don't wash your feet, you have no part with me," Jesus replied. Noting the sincerity in Jesus' voice, Peter relented and said, "LORD, not only my feet, but wash my hands and my head as well." But, Jesus responded by saying, "A person who has had a bath only needs to wash his feet, and then his whole body is clean. And, you are all clean, except one." As he said these words, he glanced toward Judas, because he knew that he would betray him.

When he had finished washing their feet, he put his clothes back on and returned to his place at the table. He asked them, "Do you understand what I have done to you? You call me, 'Teacher' and 'LORD,' and you are right in doing so, for that is what I am. But, if I am your LORD and Teacher, and I have washed your feet, then you should also wash one another's feet. For I have given you an example, that as I have done to you, you should also do to one another."

"Truly, truly I tell you, the servant is not greater than his master; neither is a messenger greater than the one who sent him. If you know these things, then you will be blessed if you do them. I am not referring to all of you. I know whom I have chosen. But this Scripture needs to be fulfilled, *'He that eats bread with me has lifted up his heel against me'*. I am telling you now before it happens, so that when it does come to pass, you may believe that I am he. I tell you the truth, whoever receives the one I send also receives me."

Sorrowfully, and with choked up emotion, Jesus said, "I tell you that one of you is going to betray me." Then the disciples began to stare at one another, wondering which one of them he meant. Now there was one disciple which leaned on Jesus' bosom named John, whom Jesus loved dearly; Peter nudged him and whispered, "Ask him which one of us he means." Turning to Jesus, John asked, "LORD, who is it?" Jesus answered, "It is the one to whom I give this piece of bread after I dip it in the dish." After he dipped the morsel, he gave it to Judas Iscariot, the son of Simon. As soon as Judas received it, Satan entered his heart. Then Jesus said to him, "What you must do, do it quickly." Immediately, Judas left the house, fearing reprisal. No one knew why Jesus had said that to him. Some thought that since Judas was the treasurer, he was being sent to buy those things that were needed for the Feast, while some of the others thought that he was supposed to give something to the poor. Then Jesus said to them, "Now is the Son of Man glorified, and G-d is glorified in him. If G-d is glorified in him, G-d shall also glorify him in himself, and will glorify him at once. Little children, I will only be with you a short while. You will look for me; and what I said to the Jews, I'm also telling you now: 'Where I am going, you cannot come.'"

Then Peter asked him, "LORD, where are you going?" "Where I am going you cannot come now," Jesus replied. "But, you'll follow me afterwards." Once again Peter asked, "LORD, why can't I follow you now?! I will lay my life down for you!" "Will you lay down your life for me?" Jesus asked. "Most assuredly I tell you, the rooster will not crow until you have denied me three times."

Raising his hand to stop Peter's rebuff, Jesus said to them, "Don't let your   hearts be troubled.   You believe in G-d? Then also believe in me. In my Father's house there are many mansions: if it wasn't so, I would have told you. And if I go and prepare a place for you, I will return and take you back with me; so that where I am, you may be also. You know where I am going, and you also know the way." Then Thomas said to him, "LORD, if we don't know where you're going, how can we know the way?" In response, Jesus said, "I am the way; I am the truth; and I am the life. No one can come to the Father except through me. If you have known me, you would have known my Father also. From now on, you do know him, and have seen him." Then Philip said to him, "LORD, show us the Father, and it will suffice us." "Have I been with you for such a long time, Philip, and you still don't know me?" Jesus asked. "He that has seen me has seen the Father; so how can you say, 'Show us the Father'?

Don't you believe that I am in the Father, and that the Father is in me? The words that I speak to you, I don't speak by my own volition. The Father that dwells in me, he does the works. Believe me when I say that I am in the Father, and the Father is in me; or else believe me because of the miracles. Truly, truly I say to you, he that believes on me, the miracles that I do shall he do also; and even greater miracles than these will he do because I am returning to my Father. Whatever you ask in my name, I will do it, so that my Father may be glorified in the Son. If you ask anything in my name, I will do it."

"If you love me, keep my commandments. And I will pray to the Father, and he will give you another Comforter who will abide with you forever, even the Spirit of Truth. The world cannot receive him because it cannot see him, nor does it know him. But you know him; for he dwells with you and shall be in you. I won't leave you orphans; I will come to you. A little while longer, and the world will see me no more, but you will see me. And because I live, you will live also. On that day you will realize that I am in the Father, you are in me, and I am in you."

Then Judas (not Judas Iscariot) said, "LORD, why will you show yourself to us but not to the world?" "The one who has my commandments and keeps them is the one who loves me," Jesus said. "He that loves me will be loved by my Father, and I will also love him and show myself to him." Then he gave them a teaching concerning the love of G-d:

I am giving you a new command now: Love one another. As I have loved you, you also must love one another. Everyone will know that you are my disciples, if you love one another. If a man loves me, he will keep my words, and my Father will love him also, and we will come to him and make our home with him. He that does not love me will not obey my teachings.

The word which you hear is not mine, but the Father's who sent me. All these things I have spoken while I am still with you; but the Comforter, the Holy Ghost, whom the Father will send in my name, He will teach you all things and bring everything that I have taught you back to your memory.

Peace, I leave with you. My peace, that which I now give and bequeath to you, cannot be compared to that which the world gives. Don't let your heart be troubled, neither let it be afraid. You heard me say, 'I am going away' and, 'I am coming back to you'. If you really loved me, you would rejoice because I said, 'I am going to the Father:' for the Father is greater than I. And now I have told you before it happens, so that when it does occur, you might believe.

After chanting the Hallel, Jesus said, "Hereafter, I will not be talking much with you, for the Prince of this world is coming. He has no claim on me, but the world must know that I love the Father and that I do exactly what my Father has commanded me. Come now, and let us leave this place." Rising, they left the house and began to walk with him towards the Mount of Olives.

XVI.

As they continued their trek towards the Mount of Olives, Jesus went on to say, "All of you will be offended because of me tonight, for it is written: *'I will smite the Shepherd, and the sheep of the flock will be scattered abroad.'* But after I have risen, I will go before you into Galilee." Then Peter declared, "though all the others may be offended because of you, yet I will never be offended." "Most assuredly, I tell you again, before the rooster crows, you will deny me three times," Jesus replied. Angered by what Jesus said, Peter declared, "Even if I have to die with you, I will never deny you!" Then the other disciples began to make the same assertion. After a brief moment of silence, Jesus gave them these final messages:

> I am the true vine and my Father is the caretaker. He takes away from me every branch that doesn't bear fruit, and every branch that does bear fruit, He prunes, so that it may bring forth more fruit. Now, you are pruned through the word which I have spoken to you.

> Abide in me; and let me abide in you. As a branch cannot bear fruit by itself, except it remains on the vine, neither can you, unless you abide in me. I am the vine and you are the branches. He that abides in me and lets me abide in him brings forth much fruit; for without me, you can do nothing. If a man does not abide in me, he is cast out like a branch and withers away. These are the branches that are gathered

together, thrown into the fire and burned. If you abide in me, and my words abide in you, ask whatever you wish, and it will be given to you. It is to my Father's glory, that you bear much fruit, for in so doing, you show yourselves to be my disciples. As the Father has loved me, so have I loved you: continue in my love. By keeping my commandments, you will remain in my love; just as I have obeyed my Father's commandments and remain in his love.

G-d is Light, and there is no darkness in him whatsoever. If a man says that he knows G-d and doesn't keep his commandments, he is a liar, and the truth is not in him. The love of G-d is perfected in those who keep his word; and this is how one knows if he is in G-d: if a man loves the world, the love of the Father is not in him. For all that the world represents, such as the lust of the flesh, the lust of the eyes and the pride of life, these things do not originate with, or emanate from, the Father, but from the world.

The desires of the flesh are contrary to the Spirit. For example, the passions of the flesh provoke hatred, adulteries, fornication, witchcraft, envy, pretension, arguments, murders, and the like. But, the desires of the Spirit incline one's heart to works of love, peacemaking, goodness, faith, meekness and temperance.

He that says he is walking in the Light and hates his brother is walking in darkness; but, he that loves his brother abides in the Light. Whoever hates his brother is a murderer; and you know that no murderer has eternal life abiding in him.

Consider this: if a man acquires wealth and turns away from his brother who is in need, how can the love of G-d be dwelling in him? Again, if a man says, 'I love G-d,' and shows no compassion for his brother, he is a liar. Besides, how can a man say he loves G-d, whom he has never seen, when he despises his brother whom he can see? Don't say that you love your brother in word only: let the love that you show be sincere and honest; neither pretend that you love. G-d is love; and everyone who loves in sincerity of heart is born of G-d, and knows G-d. Therefore, he that doesn't love his brother does not know G-d.

No man has seen G-d at any time, however, if you love one another, G-d dwells in you and his love is perfected in you. This is how you can know for sure if you dwell in him, and he dwells in you, because he has given you his Spirit – the Spirit of Love.

I have told you these things so that my joy may be in you, and that your joy may be full. This is my commandment: Love one another as I have loved you. No one can have a greater love than this; that he sacrifices his own life for the life of his friends. You are my friends if you do whatever I command you. From now on I will not call you servants; for the servant doesn't know his master's business. Instead, I call you 'friends', for all that I have heard from my Father, I have made known to you. You have not chosen me, rather I have chosen you, and ordained you to go forth and bear fruit – fruit that will last. Then, whatever you ask of the Father in my name, he will give it to you. Again, my commandment to you is this: Love one another.

If the world hates you, keep in mind that it hated me first. If you were of the world, it would love you as its own. But since you are not of this world, and because I have chosen you out from the world, the world hates you. Remember these words: 'The servant is not greater than his master'. As they have persecuted me, they will also persecute you. If they had obeyed my teachings, they would have also obeyed yours. They will treat you this way for my name's sake, because they don't know the One who sent me. If I had not come and spoken to them, then they would have had no sin; but now they don't have any cloak for their sin. If anyone hates me, they hate my Father also. If I had not performed the miracles among them that no one else did, then they would not be guilty of sin. But now they not only have seen the miracles, but they hate both me and my Father. This comes about in order that the word might be fulfilled that is written in their Law, 'they hated me without cause'.

When the Comforter comes, the Spirit of truth, whom I will send to you from the Father, he will testify of me. And you also must testify, because you have been with me from the beginning. I have told you these things so that you would not be offended. They are going to expel you from their synagogues. Yes, the times are coming that whoever kills you will think that he is doing G-d a great service. They will do these things to you because they have not known the Father, nor me. And I have told you these things, so that when the time comes you will remember that I forewarned you about them.

I didn't tell you this at first because I was with you. Now I am returning to the One who sent me. Sorrow has filled your heart ever since I have said these things to you. Nevertheless, I tell you the truth: it is for your own good that I am going away. Unless I go away the Comforter will not come to you; but if I go, I will send him to you. When He comes, he will reprove the world of guilt in regard to sin, righteousness and judgment. He will rebuke the world for sin because they don't believe in me. He will reprimand them for righteousness because I am returning to the Father where they will not see me any longer. Regarding judgment, it is because the prince of this world is judged.

I have many things to say to you, but you can't bear them now. However, when He, the Spirit of truth comes, he will guide you in all truth. He will not speak of his own accord. He will declare what he hears, and will testify of things to come. He will glorify me. He will receive from me and then show it to you.

Everything that the Father has is mine. That is why I said the Spirit will take from me and show it to you. In a little while you won't see me anymore; and then after a short time you will see me again because I'm going to the Father.

Then the disciples began to inquire among themselves as to the meaning of this statement, but it was apparent that no one understood. However, Jesus knew they wanted to ask. "Are you asking one another what I meant what I said, 'In a little while you will not see me anymore, and then after a short time you will see me again'?" Jesus asked. "I tell you, truthfully, you will weep and mourn, but the world will rejoice. You will be filled with sorrow, but your sorrow will be turned to joy."

"When a woman is in labor, she is in anguish because her time has come to deliver. However, as soon as the child is born, she no longer remembers the pain because she is filled with joy over the birth of her child. So it is with you now, for you are filled with grief. But when I see you again, your heart will rejoice; and no one will be able to take away your joy. In that day you will ask me for nothing. I tell you the truth, my Father will give you whatever you ask for in my name. Until now, you have asked for nothing in my name. Ask, and you will receive, so that your joy may be complete. Thus far, I have spoken to you in proverbs, but the time is coming when I will tell you about the Father plainly. In that day, you will ask for something in my name, and I will not say to you that I will pray to the Father for you. For the Father, himself, loves you because you love me and believe that I came out from G-d. **I came out from the Father and have come into the world; now I am leaving the world and I am returning to the Father."**

Then the disciples said to him, "Now you're speaking clearly, rather than in proverbs! Now we're sure that you know all that is in our heart, and that it's unnecessary for us to ask you any questions. Because of this, we know that you have come from G-d." "Do you believe now?" Jesus asked. "The time is coming, and has already come, when you will be scattered. Every one of you will return to his own house and leave me alone. Yet, I am never alone, for my Father is always with me. I have told you these things, so that in me you may have peace. In this world you will have trouble. But be cheerful: I have overcome the world." After Jesus said these things, he lifted up his eyes to heaven and prayed:

Father, the time has come. Glorify your Son, so that your Son may glorify you. You have given him power over all people, so that he might give eternal life to all that you have given him. Now this is eternal life: that they may know you, the only true G-d, and Jesus Christ, whom you have sent.

I have glorified you on the earth. I have finished the work that you gave me to do. Now, Father, glorify me with your own self; with the glory that I had with you before the world began. I have revealed your name to those whom you have given me out of the world. They were yours, and you gave them to me. They have obeyed your word. Now they know that whatever you have given me comes from you. For I gave them your words and they accepted them. They know with all certainty that I came out from you, and they also believe that you have sent me.

I pray for them. I am not praying for the world, but for those you have given me, for they are yours. All I have is yours, and all you have is mine, and I am glorified through them. I will not be in the world much longer, but they will continue here in the world. I am coming to you, Holy Father. Protect them by the power of your name so that they may be one, just as we are one. While I am with them in this world, I keep them secure in your name. None has been lost except the one doomed to destruction, by whom the Scripture would be fulfilled. I am coming to you now, but I say these things while I am still in the world, so that they may have the full measure of my joy within them. I have given them your word and the world has hated them, because they are not of the world any more than I am of the world. My prayer is not that you take them out of the world but that you protect them from the evil one. They are not of this world, even as I am not of it. O sanctify them by your truth. Your word is the truth.

As you sent me into the world, I have sent them into the world. For their sakes I sanctify myself, that they too may be sanctified through the truth. My prayer is not for them alone. I pray also for those who will believe in me through their message. I pray that they all may be one, Father, just as you are in me and I am in you. May they also be one in us, so that the world may believe that you have sent me. I have given them the glory that you gave me, that they may be one, as we are one: I in them and you in me. May they be unified, so that the world may know that you have sent me and have loved them even as you have loved me.

Father, I want those you have given me to be with me where I am. I want them to see the glory that you gave me before the creation of the world, because you loved me. Righteous Father, the world has not known you: I know you, and these know that you have sent me. I have confessed your name to them, and will continue to make you known, in order that the love you have for me may be in them and that I myself may be in them.

After concluding his prayer, Jesus and his disciples crossed the brook Kedron and entered the Garden of Gethsemane. When they reached a certain point, he turned to his disciples and said, "Sit here while I go over there and pray." Then he took Peter, James and John, and withdrew from them about a stone's throw away. As they walked, Jesus was filled with a deep sorrow. He said to the three, "My soul is overwhelmed with sorrow, even to the point of death. Wait here and watch with me. Pray that you don't enter into temptation." Leaving them there, he went on a little further and prostrated himself in prayer.

As he was about to open his mouth to pray, Lucifer presented himself carrying a black cup in his hand. He said to Jesus," Take this cup of the LORD's fury and drink it." Jesus withdraws his hand refusing to obey the devil and petitions the Father. "Let my prayer be set before you as incense, O' G-d" Jesus began. "I have been afflicted and ready to die since my youth. O my Father, if it be possible, let this cup pass from me. However, not as I will, but as you will." Jesus takes the cup and drinks its contents.

After one hour of intense physical suffering, Jesus arose and walked over to his disciples and found them asleep. He awakened Peter and said to him, "Could you not watch with me for one hour? Watch and pray that you enter not into temptation. The Spirit is willing indeed, but the flesh is weak."Then he turned and went away the second time. Lucifer approached him again saying, "Take this cup of fear and trembling and drink all of it." Lifting up his voice in prayer, Jesus said, "I will praise you, O LORD my G-d. I will praise you with all my heart, and I will glorify your name forever. O my Father, if this cup may not pass away from me, except I drink it; your will be done." Jesus stretches out his hand, takes the cup and drinks its contents. After one hour of intense spiritual conflict, Jesus arises and returns to his disciples. Once again he finds them asleep. This time he leaves them and returns to pray the third time. Once again Lucifer returns with the third cup. He says to Jesus, "Take this cup of desolation and drink all of it." Again Jesus turns to the father saying, "You have known my reproach, my shame and my dishonor. My adversaries are all before you. Reproach has broken my heart, and I am heavy hearted. Did I not weep for him that was in trouble? Was my soul not grieved for the poor? O' that my anguish could be weighed, and my misery placed on the scales! Surely, it would outweigh the sand of the sea. I am feeble and utterly crushed. I groan in the anguish of my heart. LORD, all my desire is before you. My groaning is not hidden from you. Father if this cup may pass from me; but, not as I will, but your will be done." As he prayed in the anguish of his heart, the sweat that fell from his head were like drops of blood falling to the ground. He took the cup and drank its contents. After one hour of deep emotional and heart wrenching torment an Angel appeared to him from heaven and strengthened him. "Peace be to you," the Angel said. "Be strong. Yes, be strong. There is one more cup to drink, and you will need your strength." Then Jesus arose and returned to his disciples. Finding them asleep, he said, "Continue to sleep and rest. Be aware that the time has come: The Son of Man is betrayed into the hands of sinners."

Moments later, Jesus heard the sound of rushing footsteps. Looking up, he could see the burning lights of a great many torches. Arousing his disciples, he said, "Get up, and let us go! Look! Here comes my betrayer." While he was still speaking, Judas Iscariot approached them, accompanied by a multitude of men sent with him by the chief priests and elders of the people. They were carrying torches, lanterns and weapons. Judas had devised a plan and arranged a signal with them: "We will come upon him late at night, when he is weary and weak. Then all the people that are with him will flee. The one I kiss is the man; arrest him." Walking up to Jesus, he kissed him and said, "Hail, Master!" Jesus replied, "Friend, why have you come? Have you betrayed the Son of Man with a kiss?"

Knowing what was about to befall him, Jesus took a step forward and spoke to the multitude. "Whom do you seek?" He asked. "Jesus of Nazareth," they replied. He said, "I am he." As soon as Jesus said, 'I am he,' they went backward and fell to the ground. This occurred that another Scripture would be fulfilled:

> When the wicked, my enemies and foes came upon me to eat up my flesh, they stumbled and fell. Yes, they are fallen beneath my feet. You armed me with strength for battle, and made my enemies bow at my feet.

"Whom are you seeking?" Jesus asked again. "We seek Jesus of Nazareth!" They replied. Once again, Jesus said to them, "I told you that I am he. Therefore, if you are looking for me, let these go on their way.' (He said this so that the words he had spoken would be fulfilled: 'I have lost none of those that you have given me."

When his disciples realized what was happening, they turned to him and said, "LORD, shall we strike with the sword?" But without waiting for an answer, Peter lunged forward and struck Malchus, the servant of the high priest, and cut off his right ear. Stepping between Malchus and Peter, Jesus rebuked Peter sharply. "Put your sword back in its sheath!" Jesus commanded. "The cup my Father has given me to drink, shall I not drink it? For all those who use the sword shall perish by the sword! Don't you think that I can pray to my Father right now, and he would immediately give me more than twelve legions of angels? How then can the Scriptures be fulfilled that say it must be this way? Allow this much!"

Jesus turned around, touched Malchus' ear and healed him. Then he turned his attention to the crowd: "Are you coming to capture me, like you would a thief, with swords and spears? Every day I sat in the Temple teaching, and you never laid a hand on me. But this is your hour, and his, the Prince of darkness." As the man approached Jesus to take him captive, his disciples deserted him and fled. All of this took place in fulfillment of the writings of the prophets:

'Awake, O sword, against my Shepherd. Smite the Shepherd and the sheep will be scattered.'

While his captors were binding his hands together, Jesus fastened his eyes on Judas and said to him, "If it was an enemy that dishonored me, I could have accepted it. If it was one that hated me, I could have avoided him. But it was you, my companion and close friend: one with whom I enjoyed sweet fellowship as we walked to the Temple of G-d together." Then the men shoved him forward and brought him to Annas, the father-in-law to Caiaphas, the high priest. After making a mockery of him, Annas sent him to Caiaphas where the scribes and elders were eagerly awaiting him.

XVII.

As Jesus stood before the Sanhedrin, listening to the testimony made against him by false witnesses, he reflected upon the words of the prophets:

> *Why are the nations in an uproar? Why do the people mumble in vain? The kings of the earth stand up, and the rulers take counsel together against the LORD, and against his anointed.*

> *They say, 'Let us break their bands asunder, and cast away their cords from us.'*

> *But he that sits in heaven laughs. The LORD has them in derision. He will speak to them in his wrath, and frighten them in his sore displeasure. Truly, it is I that have established my King upon Zion, my holy mountain.*

Simon Peter and another disciple followed Jesus to Caiaphas's house. The disciple that had accompanied Peter was known to the high priest, therefore he was able to enter his courtyard. Peter, however, had to wait outside until after the disciple obtained permission from the guard, and she let Peter in. Upon entering the court Peter went in and sat by the fire with the other servants, both to keep warm and to see what would happen to Jesus. But, as he stood there warming himself, he became a little uncomfortable when he discovered that the guard's eyes were fixed on him. Finally, she spoke up and said, "This man was also with him!" Pretending to be startled by her words, Peter raised up abruptly. "Are you not one of this man's disciples also?" She asked. "I am not!" Peter explained. "Woman, I don't even know him! I don't know what you're talking about!" Then Peter stormed away in a mock display of rage and went out onto the porch.

The chief priests, together with the Sanhedrin, were looking for witnesses against Jesus, witnesses whose testimonies would provide them with enough information to condemn him to death. Although many came forward, they could not find two that agreed with each other so they might convict him. Finally, two men came in; one of whom declared, "This fellow said, 'I am able to destroy the Temple of G-d and rebuild it in three days.'" The other said, "He has appointed prophets to proclaim to the people at Jerusalem, 'There is a king in Judah!'"

Turning his attention to the Almighty, Jesus prayed silently:

> *False witnesses are rising up and accusing me of things I never did. They have spoken many lies against me and I don't even know the things they are speaking of. They reward me with evil for the good that I did for them." Fastening his eyes on a particular witness, Jesus continued: "I treated him as though he was my friend or brother. But in my adversity they rejoice and gather against me. They have no cause to contend with me. For my love, they are my adversaries. Nevertheless, I give myself to prayer. This day is a day of trouble, rebuke and blasphemy. You have seen all their vengeance and their mischief against me, and you have heard their condemnation, O LORD. You listened to them, as they devised their plan to hurt me. But I am acting like a deaf mute. I am not opening my ears, nor my mouth, for I know that*

you will redeem my soul from the power of the
grave, then receive me to glory.

Caiaphas stood up and spoke to Jesus: "Don't you have anything to say? What is the truth concerning these things they're saying against you?" But, Jesus held his peace. Then Caiaphas questioned Jesus about his disciples and his teaching. "I have spoken openly to the world," Jesus replied. "I always taught in the synagogues or at the Temple, where all the Jews congregate. I have said nothing in secret, so why question me? Ask those who heard me. Surely they know what I said." When Jesus said this, one of the officers struck him in the face with the palm of his hand. "Is this the way you answer the high priest?" He bellowed. Then Jesus answered him, "If I have said something evil, bear witness of the evil. But if I have spoken the truth, why do you strike me?" "Because you have mocked me!" Caiaphas shouted. "I adjure you by the living G-d that you tell us whether or not you are the Messiah, the Son of G-d!"

Jesus said, "You have spoken. Nevertheless, I say to all of you; hereafter, you will see the Son of Man sitting on the right hand of power and coming in the clouds of heaven." Ripping his clothes, and turning to face the Sanhedrin, Caiaphas cried out: "He has spoken blasphemy! What do we need with any more witnesses? You have heard his blasphemy, what do you think?" All at once, they stood up and shouted, "He is worthy of death!"

Meanwhile, Peter was waiting on the porch when another maid saw him and cried out to the others, "This fellow was also with Jesus of Nazareth!" Pointing to Peter, she said, "You are one of his disciples!" Immediately, Peter shouted, "I am not! I don't even know him!" Then he walked away from her and returned to the place where the servants of Caiaphas were warming themselves.

Inside the chamber, the guardsmen that were holding Jesus began to mock him and punch him repeatedly all over his face and body. Several members of the Sanhedrin also joined in the melee and began to slap his face and spit on him. Then they tied his hands behind him, blindfolded him, and began to taunt him as they struck him time and again. "Prophesy, Jesus!" One shouted; "Tell us who struck you!" "Come on, Messiah! Tell us who hit you?" Another demanded, as they continued their aggression.

As Peter warmed himself, one of the servants said to him, "Are you not also one of his disciples? Fearfully, Peter looked up and around, pretending not to know of whom the servant was speaking. Then a relative of Malchus, whose ear Peter cut off, spoke up and said, "Did I not see you in the garden with him?" Peter denied it again, saying, "No, man. I don't even know what you're talking about!" Then one of them said, "Surely you are one of them, for your accent gives you away." Then Peter began to curse and swear. "I told you that I don't know the man!" He screamed. Peter was unaware that they had just brought Jesus from the Council chamber. Immediately after he shouted, "I don't know the man," he saw Jesus; and at that same instant the rooster crowed. Upon hearing the sound of the rooster, Jesus turned his head and looked directly at Peter. Then Peter remembered the words that the LORD had spoken earlier in the evening: "Before the rooster crows today, you will deny me three times." Filled with shame and utter humiliation, he ran out and wept bitterly.

It was early in the morning, before dawn, when they led Jesus from Caiaphas to the judgment hall. However, the priests and scribes refrained from entering the hall because they were afraid they might defile themselves and be forbidden to eat the Passover. Therefore, at dawn, the chief priests and elders of the people led Jesus back to their Council chambers to question him again, even though they had already conspired with the elders of the people to have him put to death. "If you are the Messiah, tell us!" They shouted. Jesus replied, "If I tell you plainly, you will not believe. And if I ask you, you would not answer me. But, as I have already told you, hereafter, the Son of Man will be seated at the right hand of the mighty G-d." Again they asked him, "Are you the Son of G-d then?" "You say that I am," Jesus said. "What do we need with any more witnesses?" An elder asked. "We have heard him say these things ourselves!" Then they led him away to the judgment hall and delivered him to Pontius Pilate, the governor of Judea.

When Judas Iscariot saw that Jesus was condemned, he was sorry for what he had done. Wishing to repent, he went back to the priests and returned the thirty pieces of silver. "I have sinned," Judas said, "for I have betrayed innocent blood." "What is that to us? That is your blunder." They replied. Angrily, Judas threw the silver coins on the floor of the Temple, ran out and hung himself. After picking up the coins, one of the chief priests said, "It is unlawful for us to put these coins into the treasury because it is blood money, so, what should we do?" After deliberating with one another, they decided to use the money to buy the Potters Field as a burial place for foreigners. Therefore, the field was called, 'the Field of Blood'; fulfilling this prophecy of Jeremiah:

*They took the thirty pieces of silver, the value of
him that the children of Israel did appraise; and
gave them for the Potters Field, as the LORD
appointed me.*

Meanwhile, they had brought Jesus before Pontius Pilate.
Facing the priests and leaders of the Jews, Pilate asked,
"What accusation do you make against this man?" A priest
answered, "We found this fellow perverting the nation. He
forbids them to give tribute to Caesar, and says that he is
the Christ, and a King." Repressing the urge to laugh, Pilate
asked Jesus, "Are you the King of the Jews?" "You say it,"
Jesus replied. Then one of the priests said to Pilate, "If he
wasn't a criminal, we wouldn't have handed him over to
you." "I can't find any fault in this man," Pilate said.
Obviously angered, the priest declared, "He stirs up the
people all over Judea by his teaching. He started in Galilee
and has come all the way here." Pilate turned to Jesus and
said, "Do you hear all these things they're saying against
you?" When Jesus didn't answer, he marveled. Then a
thought came to him; "Is he a Galilean?" He asked. "He is a
Nazarene, from Galilee," answered the priest. Therefore,
when he heard that Jesus belonged to Herod's jurisdiction,
Pilate ordered that Jesus be taken to him. Now when Herod
saw Jesus, he was greatly pleased, because he had been
wanting to see him for a long time. Furthermore, he was
hoping that Jesus would perform some miracle for his
pleasure. Although Herod asked him many questions, Jesus
remained silent and refused to respond to any of them.
Finally, in the presence of a jeering crowd, Herod began to
make a mockery of him in hopes of arousing a response:
"Call now, if you will. Let us see if anyone answers you. To
which of the holy ones will you turn? If you were pure and

upright, surely G-d would arouse himself on your behalf. Surely, he would restore you to your rightful place and make your righteousness prosper. Listen, G-d will not cast away a perfect man; but, neither will he help the sinners!" When Jesus failed to respond, Herod shouted, "Should my questions not be answered!?" Still, Jesus maintained his silence.

Herod continued, "Is it any pleasure to the Almighty that you are a righteous man? What would he gain if you made yourself pure? If you have something to say, say it! Speak now, for I am trying to justify you!" As soon as Herod said these words, a priest stood up and interjected, "He said that he was the king; that he was the Son of G-d! Therefore, we urge the King to have this man put to death. He is corrupting the people of this City by his false teachings." In the end, they arrayed Jesus in a gorgeous robe and sent him back to Pilate. Before that day, Herod and Pilate opposed one another; but from that day forward, they became friends.

After being made aware of the return of Jesus, Pilate summoned the chief priests and elders of the people into the judgment hall. When they arrived, he came out and stood before them and said, "You have brought this man to me, charging him with perverting the people and inciting them to rebellion. I have examined him before all of you and can find no basis for these charges. Neither has Herod, for he sent him back to us. As you can see, he has done nothing to deserve death. Ever since you have brought him to me, I have found no fault in him." Thus the prophecy of the prophet Daniel was fulfilled,

They could find neither an accusation nor a fault, for as much as he was faithful. Neither was there any error or sin found in him.

"You take him and judge him according to your Law!" Pilate decreed. "It isn't lawful for us to put any man to death!" They shouted. After this exchange of words, Pilate turned and went back into the judgment hall and had Jesus brought before him. Looking steadfastly upon him, Pilate said, "So, you are the King of the Jews." Jesus replied, "Do you say this of your own accord, or did others tell you this concerning me?" "Am I a Jew?" Pilate bellowed. "Your own nation and the chief priests have handed you over to me! What have you done?" Then Jesus said to him, "My kingdom is not of this world. If my kingdom was of this world, my servants would fight to prevent my arrest by the Jews. But my kingdom is not from here." "Are you a king then?" Pilate asked. "You say that I'm a king." Jesus replied. Gesturing to his hapless predicament, Jesus said, "I was born to this end. It was for this reason that I came into the world, to bear witness of the truth. Everyone who listens to my voice sides with the truth." Turning away from him in utter bewilderment, Pilate returned to the waiting Jews muttering, "What is truth?"

While he was in the judgment hall with Jesus, the chief priests and scribes spoke to the leaders of the people saying: "This man is worthy to die because he has prophesied against this City. You have heard him with your own ears." And with many such words they succeeded in stirring up the elders. Then they persuaded the multitude to demand that Pilate release Jesus Barabbas, a notorious prisoner, and to condemn Jesus of Nazareth to death. (At the Passover Feast the governor was known to release one prisoner to the people, whomever they wanted.)

When Pilate emerged from the judgment hall, he said to them: "I can find no fault in him at all. Therefore, my decision is to chastise him and release him." (Raising his hands to silence the crowd's outburst, Pilate continued): "However, you have a custom, that I should release one prisoner to you at the Passover. Do you want me to release the King of the Jews?" "Do away with this man, and release Barabbas to us!" They shouted.

At that moment a messenger sent by Pilate's wife arrived. He approached Pilate and said, "I have a message from your wife Sir. She said, 'Have nothing to do with that just man: for I have suffered many things today in a dream because of him.'" Again, Pilate asked the Jews, "Whom would you have me release to you, Jesus Barabbas, or Jesus, the Messiah?" "Release Barabbas to us, not this man!" They shouted. (Pilate wanted to release Jesus of Nazareth because he knew that the Jews had handed him over out of jealousy). "Why?" Pilate asked. "What evil has he done? I haven't found any cause for condemning him to death. Therefore, I will chastise him and let him go." Motioning the guards to take Jesus away, Pilate reentered the judgment hall. Outside, the crowd continued to chant and shout, "Crucify him! Crucify him!"

The soldiers tied Jesus between two columns and proceeded to give him thirty-nine lashes with a scourge. (A scourge was a band of leather straps inlaid with pieces of glass and jagged rocks. Each lash made grievous wounds in the man's flesh and as the scourge would be withdrawn to deliver another blow, pieces of the victim's flesh and blood would cling to it). One soldier made a crown out of thorns and pressed them into his scalp, and another wrapped a purple robe about him. Then bowing before him in mock worship they began to shout, "Hail, King of the Jews! Hail to the King!" As they rose from their knees, they took the staff and began to hit him across the face and head. In so doing, these Scriptures were fulfilled:

> *They shall strike the Judge of Israel upon the cheek.*
> *He gives his cheek to him that strikes him: he is*
> *filled with reproach.*

After the captain of the guard brought Jesus back into the hall, Pilate went out to the Jews and said, "Look, I am bringing him out to you to let you know that I find no fault in him." When Jesus came out wearing the crown of thorns and the purple robe, Pilate said to them, "Look at the man!" Then the chief priests and scribes began to shout, "Crucify him! Crucify him!" "You take him and crucify him!" Pilate cried out. "As for me, I can't find fault with him." However, the Jews insisted, saying, "We have a law, and in accordance with that law he must die, because he claimed to be the Son of G-d!" When Pilate heard this, he was even more afraid. He returned to the judgment hall and had Jesus brought to him. "Where are you from?" Pilate asked. But Jesus gave him no answer. "Are you refusing to speak to me? Don't you know that I have the power to crucify you and the power to release you?" Jesus replied, "You could have no power at all against me if it wasn't given to you from above. Therefore, the one who handed me over to you has the greater sin."

Returning to the waiting crowds, Pilate wanted to release him, but they immediately began to cry out, "If you let this man go, you are not Caesar's friend! Whoever makes himself a king speaks out against Caesar!" Upon hearing these words, he brought Jesus out again, and sat down on the judge's seat in a place known as the Stone Pavement. It was the preparation of the Passover and nearing the noon hour. Then he said to the Jews, "Behold your King!" But the Jews began to shout even louder, "Take him away! Take him away! Crucify him!" "Shall I crucify your King?" Pilate asked. "We have no king but Caesar!" They exclaimed.

When Pilate saw that he could not prevail, but that a big commotion was being made, he asked for some water. Then, as he washed his hands before the crowd, he said, "I am innocent of the blood of this just person. You see to it." "Let his blood be upon us and upon our children! They shouted; consenting to his death. After washing his hands, Pilate decreed that the demands of the people be honored. He released Jesus Barabbas, who had been thrown into prison for sedition and murder, and handed Jesus of Nazareth over to be crucified.

The soldiers took Jesus back into the Praetorium, where they gathered the entire garrison of soldiers around him. They stripped him of his clothing, put a scarlet robe around him, and put a staff in his right hand. One by one, they began to bow before him in mock worship, saying, "Hail, King of the Jews!" As they rose from their knees, they spit in his face, took the staff from his hand and hit him on the head repeatedly. After all this, his face and head swollen and bruised beyond recognition, they began to pull at his beard and ripped the hairs from his face. Then, after what seemed like an endless period of torture, they removed the robe from him, put his own clothing back on him, and led him away to be crucified. Centuries earlier, the prophets foretold his passion with divine infallibility:

> He was oppressed and afflicted, yet he never opened his mouth.

> I gave my back to the murderers and my cheeks to them that pluck off the hair. I did not hide my face from shame and spitting.

> Now I am their song. I am their byword. They hate me. They stand back from me and spare not to spit in my face, for G-d has loosed my cord and afflicted me.

> He has torn me in his wrath, and gnashed upon me with his teeth. They have gathered themselves against me, and struck me upon the cheek reproachfully.

> Surely our diseases he did bear, and our pains he carried; whereas we esteemed him stricken, smitten of G-d, and afflicted.

> But he was wounded for our transgressions, and he was bruised because of our iniquities.

> His face was so disfigured and swollen that he hardly looked like a man, and his appearance was marred beyond any human likeness.

> The chastisement of our peace was upon him, and with his stripes we were healed. The LORD has made to rest on him the iniquity of us all. He was oppressed, though he humbled himself and opened not his mouth.

> He was like a lamb that is led to the slaughter. Like a sheep before her shearers is dumb, he did not open his mouth. Though he had done no violence, neither was any deceit in his mouth.

He was taken from the prison and from the judgment hall; but who could reason with this generation?

Physically weak, afflicted with searing pain and debilitated from a sleepless night of torture, Jesus soon fell under the weight of the cross. Immediately, the soldiers took hold of a man named Simon, of Cyrene, and compelled him to carry the cross as they led Jesus outside the City. A great company of men and women followed the procession to Calvary, many of whom began to wail and sob when they saw his face. Jesus said to them, "Daughters of Jerusalem, don't cry for me; cry for yourselves and your children. The days are coming when they will say, 'Blessed are the barren,' and, 'Blessed are the wombs that never bore children, and the breasts that never produced milk.' Then they will begin to say to the mountains and hills, 'Fall on us, and cover us!' You see my distress and are afraid, but if they do these things in a green tree, what will they do to a dry one?" As he concluded these words, a soldier shoved him forward.

At about the noon hour, a strange darkness began to appear in the distant sky; and as it began to slowly engulf the heavens over Jerusalem, many began to say that a terrible storm was coming, fulfilling yet another of the Scriptures:

It shall come to pass in that day, said the LORD, that I will cause the sun to go down at noon, and I will darken the earth in the clear day.

Struggling to keep his balance, Jesus slipped and fell to one knee. The priests and elders began to jeer at him and to mock him; but he turned a deaf ear to them and continued to speak in his heart to the Father. "My knees give way from fasting. I am disgusting to them, and when they look at me they shake their heads. When my foot slips, they jeer at me. I am ready to stop; for there is no relief from the pain. I am counted with those who go down to the pit; like a man that has no strength." Rising to his feet, Jesus continues to pray. "Even the young children despise me; but I'm like a lamb or an ox that is brought to the slaughter. They say, 'Let's destroy the tree with its fruit, and let's cut him off from the land of the living so that his name isn't remembered any longer.' My heart is pounding and my strength is failing me. My back is filled with searing pain and there is no vigor in my body." Then Jesus saw his sister standing off in the distance. "My relatives and friends are standing out of sight in the distance. They can't bear to look upon me because of my wounds. My flesh is sore and broken. No one claims to know me. They are in distress because they had put such hope in me. Now, they are filled with disappointment. O LORD; if only they knew that this was your hand, and that it was you who were doing this! LORD, your hand is lifted up, and they can't see it! But they will see it, for you will not leave my soul in the grave."

They finally reached the top of the hill, called Calvary and Golgotha, where he would be crucified. There, they removed his garments and tried to give him vinegar to drink mixed with gall, but he refused it; as it is written, 'They gave me gall for my food, and vinegar to quench my thirst'. Then a centurion said to one of his soldiers, "Bind him with these cords to the cross."

While they were securing him to the cross Pilate approached with a band of soldiers. He carried a piece of parchment in his hand which he nailed to the cross. It was written in Hebrew, Greek, and Latin, and read: "Jesus of Nazareth, the

King of the Jews." When the chief priest read it he said to Pilate, "Don't write, 'the King of the Jews,' but that, 'This man claimed to be the King of the Jews.'" Pilate responded contemptuously, "What I have written, I have written!" Abruptly, he turned away from them and left the scene.

After nailing his hands and feet to the cross the soldiers lifted the cross and set it into the hole that had been dug for it. Satisfied that he was firmly secured, they removed the cords from his arms. The sudden drop of his upper torso sent a surge of excruciating pain through his entire body and his blood began to trickle out and accumulate in small puddles at the bottom of the cross. (Two thieves were also crucified along with him, one on his right and the other to his left).

As he hung on the cross in agonizing torment, the soldiers began to divide his garments among themselves. However, when they examined his coat, (A one-piece seamless garment that had been woven from the top to the bottom) and realized that it was an expensive piece of clothing, they decided to cast dice for it. In doing so, they unwittingly took part in the fulfillment of another Scripture: 'They parted my garments between them and cast lots for my vesture'.

Jesus, in great torment, and struggling to breathe, began to pray silently for the children of Israel:

> *Holy Father hear my prayer. Whenever the children of Israel look toward this place and begin to pray; hear their prayer from heaven, your dwelling place, and forgive their sin. When your people, the children of Israel, are taken captive by their enemies because they have sinned against you; and they turn back to you again, confessing your name, and looking toward this place in hope:*

if they repent, and return to you with all their heart, and with all their soul, even though they are in the land of their enemies, then hear their prayer, and forgive all the sin of Israel.

Remember the promise that you made to their ancestors and allow them to return to this land which you have given to them for an inheritance. For they are your people, and your inheritance, which you brought forth out of Egypt, from the midst of the iron furnace.

Let your eyes be open and your ears attentive to the prayer of your servants, and to the prayers of all your people Israel. Give them all that they ask you for. For you did separate them from among all the people of the earth, to be your inheritance.

When you shut up the heavens and withhold the rains because they have sinned against you; if they pray toward this place, confess your name, and are willing to turn from their sin after you have afflicted them: hear their prayer. Hear their prayer from heaven, and forgive the sin of your servants, and of your people Israel. Cause them to learn the way in which they should walk, and let the heavens pour down rain upon your land.

If there is a famine or pestilence in the land, or, if an enemy lays siege to any of their cities; whatever the plague or sickness may be, no matter what the circumstance. Whether a prayer is made by one man, or by all of your people Israel at the same time, acknowledging the sin of their own heart, and stretching out their hands toward this place in hope: hear their prayer.

O hear their prayer from heaven, your dwelling place. Forgive them and act upon their prayer. Remove from them the famine and the pestilence, and rebuke their enemies. Give to every man according to his ways, for you know their hearts. In this way they will learn to fear you all their days.

As for the Gentile that doesn't belong to your people Israel, but comes from a far country for your namesake, listen to their prayer. Surely, they will hear of your great name, and of your strong hand, and stretched out arm. When he comes and prays toward this Temple, hear his prayer from heaven, and do according to all that the stranger asks of you. Grant them the desires of their heart. In this way all the people of the earth may know your name and fear you, as your people Israel do; and furthermore, that they may know this Temple is called by your name.

Remember your servants Abraham, Isaac, and Jacob when you see the stubbornness of these people, and remember your promises of old; for they are still your people which you have redeemed with your arm this day. Let this prayer remain before you forever, that your mercy may be upon all who call upon you in their necessity.

When Jesus saw his mother and the disciple John standing before him, he said, "What a pity, my mother! You had to give birth to me, a man of strife and contention to the whole earth! Woman, look at your son!" Then Jesus focused his eyes on John and said, "Behold, your mother!" From that day forward, until the day of her death, John assumed responsibility for Mary's well-being.

Looking at the crowd of priests and scribes that had gathered to witness his suffering, Jesus continued in silent prayer:

"They look at me with gaping mouths like hungry lions. I am poured out like water and all my bones are out of joint. My strength is gone and my tongue is cleaving to the roof of my mouth. I am near death. They have pierced my hands and my feet. I can count all my bones. They are all looking and staring at me. My garments have they divided among themselves and they have cast dice for my coat."

Then in a loud voice Jesus said "Be merciful, Father, and forgive them; for they don't know what they are doing."

To the crowd, the noise of thunder echoed in the heavens, but to Jesus, hearing the voice of his Father gave him new strength; for G-d said, "I have heard your prayer, and I have seen your tears. I have sworn, and I will not repent, 'You are a priest forever after the order of Melchizedek.' On the third day you shall ascend to the House of the LORD."

Then the Jews began to mock him, saying, "You! The one who said that you're going to destroy the Temple and rebuild it in three days; save yourself! If you are the Son of G-d, come down from the cross!" Another said, "He saved others, but he can't save himself!" One of the scribes joined in the mockery and said, "If he is the King of Israel, let him come down from the cross and we will believe him." Still another scoffed at him, saying, "He trusted in G-d! Let G-d deliver him now, if he will have him, especially after hearing him say, 'I am the Son of G-d.'"

When the leaders of the Jews heard these insults hurled at Jesus they began to laugh aloud and to taunt him with their disparaging insults as well, but Jesus never responded. Turning his eyes toward heaven, he continued to pray in his heart to the Father, saying: "They are all laughing me to scorn; they shake their heads, saying, 'He trusted in the LORD to deliver him. Let him deliver him, if he truly delights in him.' You have given me my heart's desire and have not withheld the requests of my lips. I asked you for this life and you gave it to me. My glory is great in your salvation. You have laid honor and majesty upon me and have granted me eternal blessings. Your right hand, O LORD, has become glorious in power. Your right hand has dashed the enemy to pieces! As for me, I will be satisfied when I awake with your likeness."

The thief that was crucified on the left of Jesus also joined in the mockery. "If you are the Christ, save yourself and us!" He sneered. Immediately, the other criminal rebuked him. "Don't you fear G-d," he said, "considering that you are under the same sentence? Our punishment is just; we are getting what we deserve: but this man has done nothing wrong!" Then he turned to Jesus and said, "LORD, remember me when you come into your kingdom." Jesus replied, "Truly, I tell you that today you will be with me in Paradise."

Jesus had reached the point where it was extremely difficult to push his feet against the cross and raise himself up a little to catch a breath. Gasping for yet another puff of air, he faintly whispered, "My throat is dry. "Managing to strain his voice a little louder, he said, "I thirst." Then he cried out, "Eli, Eli, why have you forsaken me?"

One of the elders, upon hearing these words cried out, "He is calling out for Elijah!" Immediately, one of the people ran and retrieved a sponge; filled it with vinegar, put it on a stick, and offered it up to Jesus to drink. But when the Jews saw what he was doing, they shouted to him, "Leave him be! Let's see if Elijah will come and save him!" As soon as Jesus tasted the vinegar, he said, "It is finished." In a raspy voice he cried out, "Father, into your hand I commit my spirit." Then he died, just as it was written of him: 'in the presence of all his brethren'".

In the meantime, the leaders of the Jews had petitioned Pilate to expedite the crucifixion of the condemned men by having their legs broken. Because it was the day of the Preparation, and the eve of a high Sabbath, they wanted their bodies taken down from the crosses before dark. Having given his consent, the soldiers came and broke the legs of the first thief who had been crucified with Jesus, and then those of the other. However, when they came to Jesus and realized that he was already dead, they refrained from breaking his legs. Howbeit, one of the soldiers took a spear and pierced his side causing an immediate flow of blood and water to spurt out.

Suddenly, the land began to tremble and shake: the Temple veil was torn in two from the top to the bottom, and the ground split in several places due to the eruption of a great earthquake. Even many of the graves around Jerusalem were disturbed.

When the centurion and those that were guarding Jesus saw the earthquake and the lightning they were terrified. One exclaimed, "Surely, he was a righteous man," but another said, "Truly, this was the Son of G-d!" As these events began to unfold, many more prophecies pertaining to the Messiah were being fulfilled, among which were these:

He keeps all his bones; not one of them is broken.

They will look on him whom they have pierced.

The earth shook and trembled, also the foundations of the hills were moved and shaken because G-d was angry.

Yes, he sent out his arrows and scattered them, and he shot out lightnings and discomfited them.

His body shall not remain all night upon the tree, but you shall bury him the same day.

The Passover Lamb shall not remain until the morning, nor shall a bone be broken.

Through the roaring of the thunder and the flashing of the lightning across the skies came the voice of the Father:

All of you who are around him, mourn for him. All of you who know his name, say, 'How is the strong staff and the beautiful rod broken!' The Beauty of Israel is slain upon your high places. From the soul of his foot to the crown of his head, there was no blemish in him. He left nothing undone of all that I commanded Moses.

O Israel, do you not know that a great Prince has fallen today in your land? Was he not the most honorable of the three? Though he was tortured, he, being full of compassion, forgave their iniquity instead of destroying them. How many times he restrained his anger and did not stir up all his wrath, because he considered in his heart that they were only flesh and showed them mercy.

He redeemed them in his love. Still he was numbered with the transgressors; for he bore the sin of many and made intercession for the sinners. O' how his soul was grieved for the misery of Israel!

Yes, he loved the people. He turned many away from their sin as he walked with me in peace and equity. The law of truth was in his mouth and iniquity could not be found in his lips. Therefore, to him and to his seed after him will I give my covenant of peace, even the covenant of an everlasting priesthood. I will give it to him and to his descendants because he was zealous for the honor of his G-d and made an atonement for the children of Israel.

Hear O Israel! The life of the flesh is in the blood, and I have given it for you upon the cross. It is the blood that makes atonement for the soul. By the blood of my covenant have I blotted out your transgressions and have forgiven your sin. Return to me, for I have redeemed you!

Unknown to those standing by, something miraculous was happening to Jesus. Rising out from his bosom was   the revolving pillar of fire,   the Right Hand of G-d as in the beginning. The pillar began to rise, up, up, past the dark clouds and into space. The Right Hand of G-d stood in the open expanse of space momentarily as if awaiting instructions. Then the pillar of fire moved toward the earth. A white glowing aura surrounded it. Immediately, black figures, demon types, some with pointed wings were being expelled from the earth. Thousands of them were cast out. The last character, Lucifer, was forcefully hurled out from the earth into the depths of space. The entire earth was cleared of all evil and covered in light, the life blood of Jesus.

In his anger, Lucifer stood in the midst of the darkness and hurled his threats toward the Light. "I will never give up the fight! I will destroy as many souls as you attempt to save! I will convert them back to me! I will turn the earth against each other until they all kill one another! I will reclaim what you have taken from me!

Then G-d spoke from the heavens saying,

O' enemy of all righteousness, your destructions have come to a perpetual end. You are defeated. You shall roam the earth as a roaring lion seeking whom you may devour. Yet, if they call on my name, I shall deliver them from your teeth. It is the blood that makes atonement for the soul. By the blood of my covenant I have blotted out all transgressions and have forgiven all sin and offenses in all the earth. There is none you can claim for your own. By my own right hand have I done it and brought salvation to all who will believe in me on the earth.

Sing O' heavens, for the LORD has done it! The LORD has redeemed Jacob and glorified himself in Israel! I swore to David in truth and will not turn away from it. I said to him, 'Out of the fruit of your loins will I set one upon your throne, and cause your throne to be established forever. Your throne will be established in mercy, and he will sit upon it in the tabernacle of David, judging, seeking judgment, and promoting righteousness.' I have appointed him to be the ruler over Israel and Judah, and he will wave the sheaf before the LORD so that it will be accepted on your behalf. On the morning after the Sabbath the priest will wave it.

Looking upon his only begotten Son, G-d said, I will make your name to be remembered throughout all generations. Therefore, the people will praise you forever and ever. Your dominion will extend from sea to sea, even to the ends of the earth.

As the evening approached, Joseph, a wealthy Pharisee from Arimathea and a disciple of Jesus, who was widely regarded as a wise counselor, went to Pilate and asked that the body of Jesus be released to him. Though he was a member of the Sanhedrin, he did not agree with their decision and action against Jesus in condemning him to death.

With Pilate's permission, Joseph returned to Calvary and, accompanied by Nicodemus, took the body down from the cross. This was the same Nicodemus who had come to Jesus at night. Nicodemus carried a mixture of myrrh and aloes weighing about seventy-five pounds with him to the crucifixion site. Together, they anointed the body of Jesus and carefully wrapped his body in a linen cloth.

After their preparations were complete, they carried him to a tomb owned by Joseph in a nearby garden. The tomb had been dug just a few days earlier and no one had yet been buried in that sepulcher. They laid Jesus in the tomb, rolled a large stone over the mouth, and then went on their way. But Mary, the mother of Jesus, and Mary Magdalene, who had accompanied them to the tomb, remained there for a little while longer to weep and to mourn his death.

XVIII.

The day after the high Sabbath, the chief priests and the Pharisees went to Pilate. "Sir," they said, "we remember that while that deceiver was still alive he said, "After three days I will rise again.' We beseech you to set a guard over the sepulcher and to make it secure until the third day. Otherwise, his disciples may come and steal the body, then tell the people that he has been raised from the dead. That would make this last deception worse than the first!" Then Pilate answered, "You have a guard. You go and make the tomb as secure as you know how." Therefore, they went and made the sepulcher secure by sealing the stone and posting twenty-four hour guards over it. For three days and three nights there was an eerie quiet over Jerusalem.

The setting of the sun not only signaled the end of the Sabbath and the beginning of a new week, but it would set the stage for the beginning of a new era. For as Jonah was three days and three nights in the belly of the whale, so also was Jesus, the Messiah of G-d, in the grave three full days and nights. At the appointed hour the ground began to shake and tremble like the eruption of another earthquake; for an angel of the LORD descended from heaven and rolled back the stone from the sepulcher. When the guards saw him they were terrified and fainted at his presence.

Immediately, there was movement under the linen cloth: Jesus, the Christ of G-d, came to life. As he stood to his feet in the tomb, a magnificent light shone around him. Its splendor was like a beautifully polished diamond brandishing a magnificent spectrum of rainbow like colors. Raising his arms and his eyes toward heaven, Jesus said, "O' LORD, you have brought up my soul from the grave and have delivered me from the lowest hell. Now will I rise: now will I be exalted."

After his resurrection, many of the graves were opened in Israel, and many of the saints came out of their graves and were seen by many; even as it was written, 'your dead men shall live, and together with my dead body shall they arise'.

Mary Magdalene, Joanna, and Mary the mother of James went to the tomb of Jesus just before dawn to anoint his body with the spices they had prepared. As they walked along, they wondered aloud if the guards would be gracious to them and roll the stone away from the tomb so they could minister to him. But when they arrived at the tomb and found the stone had already been removed and the guards were gone, they were greatly perplexed. Once they looked inside and realized that the body of Jesus was not there, they immediately turned and ran back to inform the disciples of their discovery.

Mary Magdalene spoke excitedly, saying, "They have taken the LORD out of the sepulcher, and we don't know where they've taken him!" Without delay, Peter and John arose and ran to the tomb. John, being swifter than Peter, ran ahead and reached the tomb first. He looked in and saw the linen cloths lying upon the slab, but he did not go in. When Peter arrived, both he and John entered the tomb and took notice that the linen cloths were lying separate from the napkin that had been around Jesus' head. Taking into consideration that the napkin was neatly folded together and set in a place by itself, they surmised that this was not the work of body snatchers. Nevertheless, being convinced that he was not in the tomb, they departed for their own homes greatly bewildered; for as yet they did not know the Scripture that Jesus must rise again from the dead. However, Mary remained at the gravesite weeping and mourning for Jesus.

Again, Mary stooped down and looked into the tomb. This time she saw two angels in white apparel sitting there, one at the head, and the other at the feet of the slab where Jesus had been placed. They said to her, "Woman, why are you crying?" "Because they have taken away my LORD, and I don't know where they have put him," Mary replied. But when she realized that she was talking with an angel, Mary, and the women that were with her, bowed their heads to the ground in fear. Then the Angel said, "Why are you seeking one who is alive among the dead? He is not here: he has risen. Do you not remember what he said to you while he was still in Galilee? He said, 'The Son of Man must be delivered into the hands of sinful men and be crucified, and rise again on the third day.'" Then they remembered his words. "Go quickly," the Angel continued, "tell his disciples that he is risen from the dead, and that he will meet them in Galilee where they shall see him." After they spoke these words the Angels disappeared. Startled and frightened, the women who had accompanied Mary fled from the sepulcher and went to the disciples to bring them word. But the women could not comprehend the meaning of the words, "He is risen from the dead."

Moments later, as Mary rose to leave, she turned and saw a man standing there whom she thought was the gardener; but it was Jesus. "Why are you crying?" He asked. "Who are you looking for?" Mary knelt before the man and said, "Sir if you have carried him away from here, please tell me where you have put him, and I will take him away." Then Jesus said to her, "Mary!" Mary's heart jumped for joy. "Rabboni!" She gleamed. "Don't touch me," Jesus said, "for I have not ascended to my Father yet. Go to my brethren and say to them, 'I am ascending to my Father and your Father, to my G-d, and your G-d. Tell them to go into Galilee; for I will show myself to them there." Full of joy and excitement, Mary returned to the disciples and told them that she had seen the LORD, and that he wanted them to go into Galilee. Despite her exuberance and persistence, the disciples did not believe her and felt that her grief was causing her to hallucinate.

Meanwhile, the soldiers who had been guarding the tomb, ran into the City and reported what had happened to the chief priests. They wasted no time convening an emergency meeting of the Council to decide on how they were going to deal with the situation. After advising the elders of the people of the gravity of the situation, they decided to give the soldiers a large sum of money to maintain their silence. They summoned the guards before the Sanhedrin and told them to say that Jesus' disciples came at night and stole the body while they were sleeping, and that if word of the matter came to the governor, and they were imprisoned, they would persuade him to set them free. So they took the money and did as they were told. To this day, this report is commonly accepted by the Jews.

On that same day, two of Jesus' disciples traveled to a village called Emmaus, which was about seven miles from Jerusalem. As they walked along the way they discussed all the events that had taken place over the past few days, unaware that Jesus, himself, was walking beside them; however, their eyes were restrained from recognizing him. When he asked them, "What are you discussing that is making you so depressed as you walk along?" One of them, named Cleopas asked him, "Are you only a visitor to Jerusalem? Don't you realize what has been going on there these last few days?" "What things?" He asked. "About Jesus of Nazareth," they replied. "He was a prophet, powerful in word and deed before G-d and all the people. The chief priests and our rulers handed him over to be sentenced to death and they crucified him. We had hoped that he was the one who was going to redeem Israel, but it's been three days now since all this took place. A couple of the women surprised us today, though. They went to the tomb early this morning, but, instead of finding his body, they had a vision of angels who said he was alive. Then some of our companions went to the tomb and found everything to be just as the women had said, for they didn't see him either." Jesus said to them, "How foolish you are, and how slow of heart to believe all that the prophets have spoken! Didn't the Messiah have to suffer these things and then enter his glory?" And then, beginning with Moses and all the prophets, he explained to them what was said in all the Scriptures concerning himself.

As they approached the village, Jesus appeared to be going on further. But, they urged him strongly, saying, "Stay with us; for it is nearly evening and the day is almost over." So he went in and stayed with them. As he sat at the table, he took the bread, gave thanks, broke it, and gave it to them. Immediately, their eyes were opened and they recognized him; but as they looked upon his countenance, he vanished from their sight. After this, they asked each other, "Were our hearts not burning within us while he talked with us on the road and opened the Scriptures to us?"

Without delay, they arose and returned to Jerusalem. When they learned of the place where the other disciples were assembled, they went to them and exclaimed, "It is true! The LORD has risen; and he has appeared to Simon!" Then the two told them what had happened on the way to Emmaus, and how Jesus was recognized by them when he broke the bread. While they were still talking about this, Jesus appeared to them all. Standing in their midst, he greeted them with this saying, "Peace be with you." Startled and terrified, they thought they had seen a ghost. But, he said to them, "Why are you troubled; and why do doubts arise in your minds? Look at my hands and my feet. It is I myself! Touch me and see; a ghost doesn't have flesh and bones, as you see I have."

After he said this, he showed them his hands and feet, yet, they still couldn't believe their eyes. Then he asked them, "Do you have any food here to eat?" They gave him a piece of broiled fish, and watched him closely as he took it and ate it in their presence.

Then he said to them, "This is what I told you while I was still with you: everything must be fulfilled that is written about me in the Law of Moses, the Prophets and the Psalms." Then he opened their minds so they could understand the Scriptures. "It is written," said Jesus, "and therefore it was necessary, for Christ to suffer and to rise again the third day. It is also necessary that repentance and forgiveness of sins be preached in his name to all nations, beginning at Jerusalem. You are witnesses of these things. For on the first day was the holy seed buried in the earth, and on the third day was the holy seed resurrected to the glory of the Father.

"I am sending the promise of my Father upon you; but wait here at Jerusalem until you are endowed with power from on high. As John baptized with water, so shall you be baptized with the Holy Ghost not many days from now." After he said these words, he breathed on each of them and said, "Receive the Holy Ghost. Whose sins you forgive, they are forgiven; and whose sins you don't forgive, they will remain."

Now Thomas (called Didymus), one of the twelve, was not with his disciples when Jesus came. Therefore, when the other disciples said to him, "We have seen the LORD!" He replied, "Unless I see the nail marks in his hands and put my finger where the nails were, and put my hand into his side, I won't believe it." A week later his disciples were in the house again, but this time Thomas was with them. Though the doors were locked, Jesus came and stood among them and said, "Peace be with you!" Then he said to Thomas, "Put your finger here; and look at my hands. Reach out your hand and put it into my side. Stop doubting and believe." Thomas said to him, "My LORD and my G-d!" Then Jesus said, "Because you have seen me, you have believed? Blessed are those who have not seen me and yet have believed."

Afterward, Jesus appeared again to his disciples by the Sea of Tiberius. It happened this way: Simon Peter, Thomas, Nathaniel, James and John, the sons of Zebedee, and two of the other disciples were together. When Simon Peter told them that he was going fishing, they all decided to go with him. But, all through the night they caught nothing.

Early in the morning, Jesus stood on the shore and called out to them, saying, "Friends, have you caught any fish?" "No," they answered, not recognizing him. Then he said, "Throw your net on the right side of the boat and you will find some." When they did, they caught so many fish that they were unable to haul the net in. Then John cried out, "It's the LORD!" As soon as Simon Peter heard him say, "It's the LORD," he wrapped his outer garment around him for he was naked, and jumped into the water. The disciples escorted the boat in, towing the net full of fish, for they were only about a hundred yards from the shore.

When they came upon the land, they saw a fire of burning coals there with fish on it, and some bread. Jesus said to them, "Bring some of the fish you have just caught." Simon Peter, after dragging the net to shore, began to separate and count the fish. It was filled with one hundred and fifty-three large fish; but even with so many the net was not torn.

Jesus said to them, "Come and eat." None of the disciples dared ask him, "Who are you?" Because they knew it was the LORD. Then Jesus took the bread and fish and gave it to them, and they all ate. This was now the third time Jesus appeared to his disciples after he was raised from the dead. When they had finished eating, Jesus took up a fish and asked Simon Peter this question: "Simon, son of Jonah, do you truly love me more than these?" "Yes, LORD," he said, "you know that I love you." Jesus replied, "Feed my lambs." Jesus asked him again, "Simon, son of Jonah, do you truly love me?" He answered, "Yes, LORD, you know that I love you." Jesus said, "Take care of my sheep." The third time, Jesus asked, "Simon, son of Jonah, do you love me?" Peter became visibly upset and hurt because Jesus had asked him the same question three times. He replied," LORD, you know all things; you know that I love you." Jesus said, "Feed my sheep.

I tell you the truth, when you were younger you dressed yourself and went where you wanted; but when you are old, you will stretch out your hands, and someone else will dress you and lead you where you don't want to go." Jesus said this to indicate the kind of death by which Peter would glorify G-d. Then Jesus said to him, "Follow me." When Peter turned and saw John following them, he asked, "LORD, what about him?" Jesus answered, "If I want him to remain alive until I return, what is that to you? You follow me." Because of this, the rumor spread among the brothers that this disciple would never die. However, Jesus didn't say that he would never die; he only said, "If I want him to remain alive until I return, what is that to you?"

Forty days after his resurrection, Jesus led his disciples out to the Mount of Olives where he lifted up his hands and blessed them. Then they asked him, "LORD, will you restore the kingdom to Israel at this time?" Jesus replied, "It is not meant for you to know the times nor the seasons which the Father has reserved for himself. But, you will receive power, after the Holy Ghost comes upon you; and you will testify of me in Jerusalem, Judea, Samaria, even to the uttermost parts of the earth. All power is given to me in heaven and in earth. Go therefore, and teach every nation. Baptize them in the name of the Father, and of the Son and of the Holy Ghost. Teach them to observe everything that I have commanded you. Listen, I am with you always, even to the end of the world."

After he spoke these words, he began to rise up from the earth. They continued to watch him until he disappeared beyond the clouds and out of their sight. As they continued to look up into heaven, two men in white apparel came and stood by them. The men spoke and said, "You men of Galilee, why are you standing here looking up into heaven? This same Jesus, who has been taken up from you into heaven shall return in the same manner as you have seen him ascend into heaven." Leaving the Mount of Olives, they returned to their home in Jerusalem where they awaited the promise of the Holy Ghost.

www.ingramcontent.com/pod-product-compliance
Lightning Source LLC
Chambersburg PA
CBHW071523040426
42452CB00008B/868